YOUR recipe could appear in our next cookbook!

Share your tried & true family favorites with us instantly at

www.gooseberrypatch.com

If you'd rather jot 'em down by hand, just mail this form to...

Gooseberry Patch • Cookbooks – Call for Recipes
PO Box 812 • Columbus, OH 43216-0812

If your recipe is selected for a book, you'll receive a FREE copy!

Please share only your original recipes or those that you have made your own over the years.

Recipe Name:

Number of Servings:

Any fond memories about this recipe? Special touches you like to add or handy shortcuts?

Ingredients (include specific measurements):

Instructions (continue on back if needed):

T0346095

Special Code: **cookbookspage**

Over ➤

Extra space for recipe if needed:

Tell us about yourself...

Your complete contact information is needed so that we can send you your FREE cookbook, if your recipe is published. Phone numbers and email addresses are kept private and will only be used if we have questions about your recipe.

Name:

Address:

City: State: Zip:

Email:

Daytime Phone:

Thank you! Vickie & Jo Ann

Mom's Best Sunday Suppers

Tried & true recipes for gathering family around the table.

Gooseberry Patch

An imprint of Globe Pequot
64 South Main Street
Essex, CT 06426

www.gooseberrypatch.com

1·800·854·6673

Copyright 2022, Gooseberry Patch 978-1-62093-484-5

Do you have a tried & true recipe...

tip, craft or memory that you'd like to see featured in a **Gooseberry Patch** cookbook? Visit our website at **www.gooseberrypatch.com** and follow the easy steps to submit your favorite family recipe. Or send them to us at:

Gooseberry Patch
PO Box 812
Columbus, OH 43216-0812

Don't forget to include the number of servings your recipe makes, plus your name, address, phone number and email address. If we select your recipe, your name will appear right along with it... and you'll receive a **FREE** copy of the book!

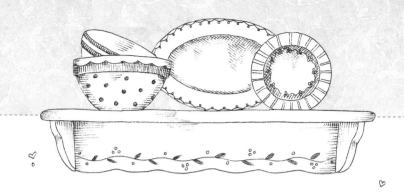

Contents

Dedication

To everyone with sweet memories of happy Sunday suppers with family at Mom's.

Appreciation

To all of you who opened up your recipe boxes and your hearts...thanks!

Sunday Dinners with Family

Mom's Best
Sunday Suppers

Simple Herb-Roasted Chicken

Elizabeth McCord
Memphis, TN

Roast chicken is one of my family's favorite cozy meals. This is the perfect recipe for a chilly Sunday afternoon! The herbs really create a delicious flavor and the apple juice ensures a juicy chicken.

4-lb. roasting chicken
3 T. olive oil
1 t. dried rosemary
1 t. dried basil
3/4 t. dried sage

3/4 t. dried thyme
1 t. salt
3/4 t. pepper
1-1/2 c. apple juice or cider

Pat chicken dry with paper towels; remove neck and giblets. Place chicken in a lightly greased roasting pan. Tuck wings under; tie legs together with kitchen string. Rub olive oil all over chicken, including inside and under the skin; set aside. Combine seasonings in a cup; sprinkle over chicken, including inside and under the skin. Pour apple juice or cider into pan around chicken. Bake, uncovered, at 350 degrees for 1-1/2 to 2 hours, until a meat thermometer inserted in the thickest part reads 165 degrees. Remove chicken to a platter; cover and let stand 10 to 15 minutes before slicing. Serves 4 to 6.

Bring out Mom's cheery fruit or flower table linens for special family get-togethers. So pretty, and they will spark conversations about other special gatherings.

Sunday Dinners with Family

Garlic & Herb Pork Loin

Courtney Stultz
Weir, KS

Family dinners are a must at our house...so are simple, healthy meals. This pork loin is very easy to make, yet is so flavorful and goes perfectly with a wide range of side dishes. We love it served with roasted sweet potatoes and fresh asparagus.

2 to 3-lb. pork loin
2 T. olive oil
2 t. cloves garlic, minced
1 t. dried rosemary
1/2 t. red pepper flakes

1/2 t. dried oregano
1/2 t. dried thyme
1/2 t. dried basil
1 t. sea salt
1/2 t. pepper

Place pork loin in a greased 3-quart casserole dish. Drizzle on all sides with olive oil; sprinkle with garlic. Combine seasonings in a cup; sprinkle over all sides of pork loin. Bake, uncovered, at 350 degrees for 35 to 45 minutes, until cooked through. Remove pork loin to a platter; let stand 10 minutes before slicing. Serves 6.

Let roasts stand for a few minutes before slicing,
so all of the savory juices can reabsorb into the meat.

Mom's Best
Sunday Suppers

Mama's Barbecued Chicken
Pamela Roberts
Chattanooga, TN

My mama created this recipe after she got married in 1958, and we're still enjoying it. The chicken is so good...it's a great comfort food.

2 to 3 lbs. bone-in chicken pieces
1 c. all-purpose flour
salt and pepper to taste
1/2 c. butter or shortening
1 c. onion, chopped
1 c. green pepper, diced
1 c. catsup

1/2 c. water
2 T. brown sugar, packed
2 T. Worcestershire sauce
2 T. vinegar
1 T. paprika
1/8 t. salt

Pat chicken dry with a paper towel. Combine flour, salt and pepper in a shallow dish; coat chicken well in mixture. Melt butter or shortening in a skillet over medium heat. Brown chicken on all sides; transfer chicken to a greased 3-quart casserole dish. To drippings in skillet, add onion and pepper; cook until lightly golden. Combine remaining ingredients in a bowl; mix well and add to onion mixture in skillet. Cook over low heat for 5 minutes to blend flavors; spoon over chicken. Bake, uncovered, at 350 degrees for one hour, or until chicken is tender and juices run clear when pierced. Serves 4 to 6.

Whether dinner is casual, served in the kitchen, or a little more formal at the dining table, be sure to add simple, special touches. Colorful napkins tied in a knot or perky blossoms tucked into a canning jar make mealtime more fun!

Sunday Dinners with Family

Grandma Frankie's Pork Chops & Rice

Beckie Apple
Grannis, AR

Grandma Frankie had nine children, so she always cooked lots of food. We all loved her special no-peek pork chop dinner.

2 c. long-cooking rice, uncooked
8 pork chops
1/4 t. salt
1/4 t. pepper
2 T. oil

1/2 c. onion, thinly sliced
4-oz. can sliced mushrooms
2 10-3/4 oz. cans cream of
   mushroom soup
3-3/4 c. water

Spread uncooked rice evenly in a greased 13"x9" deep baking pan; set aside. Season pork chops with salt and pepper. Heat oil in a large skillet; brown pork chops on both sides. Arrange browned pork chops with skillet drippings on top of rice. Arrange sliced onions and undrained mushrooms on pork chops. In a large bowl, whisk together soup and water; spoon over chicken. Cover tightly with aluminum foil. Bake at 350 degrees for one hour, or until rice and pork chops are fully cooked. Makes 8 servings.

A handy all-purpose seasoning to keep by the stove...combine 6 tablespoons salt and one tablespoon pepper in a large shaker. It's just right for sprinkling on pork chops, burgers, chicken and homestyle potatoes.

Mom's Best
Sunday Suppers

Salsa Beef Brisket

Virginia Campbell
Clifton Forge, VA

This brisket recipe is so delicious, it's always quickly devoured. Some of my family are even known to scrape the crock to get the last spoonful of the extra-yummy sauce!

16-oz. jar chunky-style salsa
   or picante sauce
1 c. onion, sliced
1 green, yellow or red pepper,
   coarsely chopped
2 c. water
1/2 c. molasses

1/2 c. brown sugar, packed
1/4 c. cider vinegar
2 T. Worcestershire sauce
3 to 4-lb. beef brisket, fat
   trimmed
cooked rice
8 soft taco shells or tortillas

In a 6-quart slow cooker, stir together all ingredients except brisket, rice and taco shells; stir to mix. Add brisket, trimming to fit if needed; turn to coat. Cover and cook on low setting for 8 to 9 hours, or on high setting for 4 to 5 hours, until brisket is fork-tender. Serve brisket sliced or shredded with warm cooked rice and warmed soft taco shells or tortillas. Makes 8 servings.

Steamy hot baked potatoes are a must with Sunday roasts. Scrub potatoes and pierce them with a fork. Rub with olive oil and roll lightly in coarse salt for yummy skins. Bake at 350 degrees for 60 minutes, placing potatoes on center oven rack and turning over once. Scrumptious!

Sunday Dinners with Family

Chicken Cacciatore

Mia Rossi
Charlotte, NC

This is a recipe my mom made for our Sunday dinners. Sometimes she added a handful of black olives to the pan. Served with pasta or rice, it only needs a chopped salad of lettuce and tomatoes to complete a delicious meal.

1 to 2 T. olive oil, divided
2-1/2 to 3 lbs. chicken pieces,
    fat trimmed
1/2 lb. sliced mushrooms
2 green peppers, sliced
3/4 c. onion, sliced
2 t. garlic, minced

28-oz. can whole peeled
    tomatoes in purée
1/2 t. dried thyme
3/4 t. salt
1/2 t. pepper
cooked spaghetti or rice

Heat oil in a Dutch oven or large skillet over medium heat. Add chicken pieces, a few at a time; brown on all sides and remove to a plate. To drippings in skillet, add mushrooms, peppers and onion; cook for 8 to 10 minutes. Add garlic; cook for about 30 seconds. Return chicken to pan. Spoon undrained tomatoes over chicken; break up tomatoes with a spoon. Sprinkle seasonings over all. Bring to a boil over medium-high heat. Reduce heat to low; cover and simmer for 40 minutes, or until chicken is very tender. Serve chicken and sauce over cooked spaghetti or rice. Makes 4 servings.

Try cavatappi pasta or extra-long fusilli pasta in a favorite recipe.
With extra twists and turns, these corkscrew-shaped pastas
hold the sauce very well...and are just plain fun to eat!

Mom's Best
Sunday Suppers

Mom's Pepper Steak

Linda Peterson
Mason, MI

One of my favorite recipes that Mom used to make. It's delicious, especially with garden-fresh green peppers and ripe tomatoes.

1-1/2 lbs. beef sirloin steak,
   1/2-inch thick, fat trimmed
Optional: 2 to 3 t. oil
1/2 t. salt, divided
1 c. onion, diced
1 c. beef broth
3 T. soy sauce
1 clove garlic, minced

2 green peppers, cut into squares
   or strips
2 T. cornstarch
1/4 c. cold water
2 ripe tomatoes, each cut into
   8 wedges
3 to 4 c. cooked rice

Cut steak into 4 to 5 serving-size pieces. Heat a large skillet over medium heat; grease skillet lightly with fat from steak (or use oil). Add steak pieces; brown well on one side. Turn steak over; sprinkle with 1/4 teaspoon salt and push to one side of skillet. Add onion to other side of skillet; cook and stir until tender. Add beef broth, soy sauce and garlic; cover and simmer for 10 minutes, or until steak is tender. Add green pepper; cover and simmer for 5 minutes. In a cup, blend cornstarch with water; gradually stir into mixture in skillet. Cook, stirring constantly, until mixture thickens and boils. Boil and stir for one minute. Add tomatoes; cook until heated through. Serve steak and sauce immediately over cooked rice. Serves 4 to 5.

Bless the food before us,
The family beside us
And the love between us,
Amen.
–Traditional

Sunday Dinners with Family

Savory Steak Strips

Connie Hilty
Pearland, TX

My mother told me this was one of the first recipes she learned to make for company. Sometimes she'd just pop some baked potatoes in the oven to serve instead of rice or noodles. However it's served, it's scrumptious!

1-1/2 lbs. beef round steak
   or chuck roast, cut into
   1-inch strips
2 to 3 T. all-purpose flour
salt and pepper to taste
2 T. olive oil
3/4 c. onion, chopped

1/2 c. celery, sliced
1/2 c. carrot, peeled and grated
8-oz. can tomato sauce
3/4 c. water
1 T. Worcestershire sauce
1 cube beef bouillon
cooked rice or egg noodles

Sprinkle beef strips with flour; season with salt and pepper. Heat oil in a large skillet over medium heat. Working in batches, add beef strips to skillet; cook and stir for 10 minutes, or until browned on all sides. Return all beef to skillet. Add onion, celery and carrot; cook and stir for 10 minutes, or until tender. Stir in remaining ingredients except rice or noodles; cook and stir until bouillon dissolves. Transfer mixture to a lightly greased 2-quart casserole dish. Cover and bake at 325 degrees for one hour and 30 minutes, or until beef is tender. Let stand 10 minutes; serve over cooked rice or noodles. Serves 4 to 6.

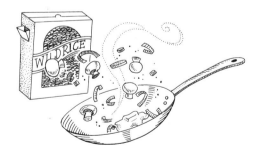

Turn a packaged wild rice mix into your own special blend in a jiffy. Sauté a cup of chopped mushrooms, onion and celery in butter until tender...you can even toss in some dried cranberries or raisins. Add the rice mix and prepare as the package directs.

Mom's Best
Sunday Suppers

Grandma's No-Peek Chicken

Sandy Coffey
Cincinnati, OH

My grandma's favorite recipe! On Sundays after Sunday school, my brother and I would visit our Grandma Carrie for a chicken dinner of some sort. Loved that day of the week! I am the proud owner of her old wooden rolling pin that's over a hundred years old.

10-3/4 oz. can cream of
   mushroom soup
10-3/4 oz. can cream of
   celery soup

1/2 c. milk
1-1/2 c. instant rice, uncooked
6 chicken breasts and/or thighs
1.35-oz. pkg. onion soup mix

Line a 13"x9" shallow baking pan with aluminum foil, leaving enough extra foil on each side to fold over and seal. In a large bowl, mix together soups, milk and rice; spread in the bottom of pan. Layer chicken on top of rice mixture, skin-side up. (Skin may be removed, if preferred.) Sprinkle soup mix over chicken. Fold foil over to seal tightly. Bake at 325 degrees for 2-1/2 hours. Do not open until serving time. Makes 6 servings.

If you have children just learning to set the table for Sunday dinner, help them draw a "proper" place setting on a big sheet of paper. Laminate their artwork and they'll have a special placemat that helps them put the silverware in the right place.

Sunday Dinners with Family

Lazy-Day Roast

Carole Schievelbein
Seguin, TX

This is a favorite recipe that I've made often. It is delicious and makes a wonderful gravy. I serve it over cooked rice, egg noodles or good old mashed potatoes. I guarantee you will love it and will make it often.

3 to 4-lb. beef chuck roast
1 c. all-purpose flour
salt and pepper to taste
2 T. oil
1-1/4 c. water

10-3/4 oz. can golden
   mushroom soup
10-3/4 oz. can French onion
   soup

Pat roast dry with a paper towel. Combine flour, salt and pepper in a shallow dish; dredge roast in mixture on all sides. Heat oil in an oven-safe skillet over medium heat; add roast and brown on all sides. In a bowl, whisk together water and soups; spoon over roast. Cover and bake at 325 degrees for 3 to 4 hours. Serves 6.

Slow-Cooker Glazed Kielbasa

Donna Lopez
Poland, OH

This is one of my 88-year-old Mom's famous recipes...she is still cooking for us every Sunday.

3 to 4 lbs. Kielbasa sausage, cut
   into chunks on the diagonal
14-oz. can whole-berry
   cranberry sauce

12-oz. bottle chili sauce
2 T. brown sugar, packed
1 T. lemon juice

Place Kielbasa in a 5-quart slow cooker; set aside. Combine remaining ingredients in a saucepan over medium heat. Stir to blend, mashing cranberries well; heat through. Spoon mixture over Kielbasa. Cover and cook on low setting for 2 to 3 hours, until heated through. Makes 6 to 8 servings.

Mom's Best
Sunday Suppers

Tuscan Chicken

Lindsey Chrostowski
Janesville, WI

This recipe is a crowd-pleaser! I like to serve it over linguine pasta,
but it's a good stand-alone dish too.

2 lbs. boneless, skinless chicken
    breasts
kosher salt and pepper to taste
1 T. extra-virgin olive oil
2 T. butter
5 cloves garlic, chopped
2 c. crimini mushrooms, sliced
1/2 c. sun-dried tomatoes,
    chopped

1 T. all-purpose flour
2 c. whole milk
1/4 t. red pepper flakes
2 c. fresh spinach, torn and
    packed
1/3 c. shredded Parmesan cheese
Optional: cooked linguine pasta

Season chicken with salt and pepper. Heat olive oil in a cast-iron skillet over medium heat; add chicken. Cook for about 10 minutes, turning occasionally, until golden. Move skillet to oven. Bake, uncovered, at 375 degrees for about 15 minutes, until chicken is cooked through. Transfer chicken to a plate; cover to keep warm. Add butter to same skillet; melt over medium heat. Add garlic; cook for about 30 seconds. Add mushrooms; sauté until golden. Add tomatoes; cook and stir for 2 minutes. Sprinkle with flour; cook and stir constantly until amber-colored. Stir in milk; bring to a simmer. Add red pepper flakes and spinach; cook until spinach wilts and sauce thickens. Stir in Parmesan cheese. Serve chicken and pasta, if desired, drizzled with sauce. Serves 4 to 6.

Cloth napkins make mealtime just a little more special.
Stitch or hot-glue fun charms to napkin rings, so family
members can identify their own napkin easily.

Sunday Dinners with Family

Chicken Noodle Casserole

Karen Wilson
Defiance, OH

A delicious creamy chicken noodle dish...cream cheese and sour cream make it extra special.

8-oz. pkg. medium egg noodles,
  uncooked
4 c. chicken broth
8-oz. pkg. cream cheese, cubed
  and softened
2 10-3/4 oz. cans cream of
  mushroom soup

1 c. sour cream
1/2 c. onion, minced
2 T. green pepper, chopped
1/2 t. salt
1/4 t. garlic salt
3 c. cooked chicken, cubed

Cook noodles in chicken broth according to package directions; drain. Place hot noodles in a bowl and add cream cheese; mix until cream cheese is melted. Add remaining ingredients except chicken; mix well. Fold in chicken; transfer to a greased 2-quart casserole dish. Cover with aluminum foil and bake at 350 degrees for one hour. Makes 8 to 10 servings.

Longing for Mom's old-fashioned homemade egg noodles? Try frozen egg noodles from your grocer's frozen food section. Thicker and heartier than dried noodles, these homestyle noodles cook up quickly in all your favorite recipes.

Mom's Best
Sunday Suppers

Crawfish or Shrimp Fettuccine *Tracy Pellegrin*
Norco, LA

I always loved this recipe that my family ate on Sundays. It can be made with either crawfish or shrimp. If it's too spicy for your taste, halve the Cajun seasoning and use plain process cheese. Serve this with a garden salad and some dinner rolls and you've got a great meal!

2 16-oz. pkgs. fettuccine pasta, uncooked
1 c. butter
1 c. onion, finely chopped
1 green pepper, finely chopped
1 stalk celery, finely chopped
2 T. garlic, minced
14-1/2 oz. can diced tomatoes with green chiles
14-1/2 oz. can chicken broth

10-3/4 oz. can cream of chicken or golden mushroom soup
Optional if using frozen seafood:
1 T. Cajun seasoning,
1 t. garlic salt
2 c. half-and-half
16-oz. pkg. Mexican pasteurized process cheese, cubed
2 lbs. cooked crawfish tails or uncooked peeled shrimp

Cook pasta according to package directions, just until tender; drain. Meanwhile, melt butter in a large skillet over medium heat. Sauté onion, green pepper and celery until softened and onion is translucent. Add garlic; sauté an additional 5 minutes. Add tomatoes with juice; sauté for 5 minutes. Stir in broth, soup and optional seasonings, if using; mix well. Add half-and-half and mix well. Add cheese; stir until completely melted. Add crawfish or shrimp; cook for 5 minutes, stirring gently. Add cooked pasta and stir gently to mix. Spoon into a greased 13"x9" lasagna pan or other deep baking pan. Cover and bake at 350 degrees for 25 minutes. Let stand 10 minutes before serving. Serves 8 to 10.

The secret to perfectly cooked pasta? Use a very large pot and plenty of cooking water, about a gallon per pound of pasta.

18

Sunday Dinners with Family

Amazing Linguine & Tomatoes
Tiffany Jones
Batesville, AR

This pasta is scrumptious...very flavorful!

16-oz. pkg. linguine pasta,
   uncooked
1 T. olive oil
1 onion, diced
1 green pepper, diced
2 14-1/2 oz. cans Italian-style
   diced tomatoes

14-1/2 oz. can vegetable broth
2 T. fresh parsley, chopped
1 T. garlic, minced
1 t. Italian seasoning
1 t. dried basil
1-1/2 t. salt
1/2 t. pepper

Cook pasta according to package directions; drain. Meanwhile, heat olive oil in a large saucepan over medium heat. Add onion and green pepper; cook until tender. Add tomatoes with juice and remaining ingredients; bring to a boil. Reduce heat to medium-low; simmer for 10 minutes. Serve tomato mixture over pasta. Serves 6.

Stovetop Macaroni & Cheese
Julie Snow
Park Rapids, MN

This is one of my family's favorites! My kids' friends always request it when they come over. I'm not a fan of baked mac & cheese, and I wanted a recipe that didn't use flour to make the cheese sauce. This is delicious as is, or you can add a pound of browned ground beef to it. We love it both ways!

2 c. elbow macaroni, uncooked
3 c. whole milk, divided
1 t. salt

1/2 t. pepper
1-1/2 c. shredded Monterey Jack
   or Cheddar Jack cheese

Combine macaroni, 2 cups milk, salt and pepper in a large skillet over medium-high heat. Bring to a boil, stirring constantly. Reduce heat to medium-low and cook, stirring often, until milk has reduced to a thick sauce. Stir in remaining milk. Continue cooking, stirring often, just until macaroni is tender and milk is reduced by half. Add cheese; cook and stir until melted and macaroni is evenly coated. Makes 4 servings.

Mom's Best
Sunday Suppers

Slow-Cooker Italian Chicken Parmesan

Emilie Britton
New Bremen, OH

A great dish to pop in the slow cooker while watching your favorite team play a big game on Sunday. Serve with spaghetti and garlic bread...yum!

1 egg, lightly beaten
1 T. water
1/2 c. seasoned dry bread
 crumbs
1/2 c. grated Parmesan cheese
1/2 t. Italian seasoning
1/4 t. salt

1/2 t. pepper
4 boneless, skinless chicken
 breasts
15-oz. jar marinara sauce
4 slices mozzarella cheese
Optional: cooked spaghetti

In a shallow bowl, whisk together egg and water. In another bowl, combine bread crumbs, Parmesan cheese and seasonings. Dip chicken into egg mixture, then into crumb mixture to coat both sides, patting to help coating adhere. Transfer chicken to a 4 or 5-quart slow cooker; spoon marinara sauce over chicken. Cover and cook on low setting for 4 to 6 hours, until chicken is cooked through. Top with cheese slices; cover and cook until cheese is melted, 10 to 15 minutes. Serve with spaghetti, if desired. Serves 4.

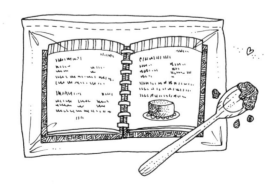

Keep a cherished cookbook clean and free of spatters.
Slip it into a gallon-size plastic zipping bag before
cooking up a favorite recipe.

Sunday Dinners with Family

Baked Herbed Chicken

JoAnn
Gooseberry Patch

*Chicken on Sunday! This is as flavorful as a whole roast chicken,
but you can add extra drumsticks for the kids. We love it with
whipped sweet potatoes and steamed broccoli.*

1/4 c. all-purpose flour	1 onion, sliced
1/2 t. salt	1/2 c. chicken broth
1/8 t. pepper	2 t. fresh parsley, snipped
3 to 4 lbs. chicken pieces	1/4 t. dried thyme
olive oil for frying	1/4 t. dried rosemary
3 whole cloves garlic, peeled	1/4 t. dried marjoram or oregano

Combine flour, salt and pepper in a large plastic zipping bag. Add
chicken to bag, several pieces at a time; shake until well coated. Add
1/4-inch olive oil, whole garlic cloves and onion to a large skillet over
medium heat. Cook chicken just until golden on both sides. Transfer
chicken and onion slices to an ungreased large roasting pan; discard
garlic. In a cup, combine chicken broth and herbs; brush over chicken.
Bake, uncovered, at 375 degrees for about 50 minutes, brushing
occasionally with broth mixture, until juices run clear and a meat
thermometer reads 165 degrees. Makes 4 to 6 servings.

Heap a vintage soup tureen with peonies or roses for
a beautiful centerpiece that's ready in a jiffy. A block of
florist's foam can hold stems in place.

Mom's Best
Sunday Suppers

Ham & Swiss Ziti

Lori Ritchey
Denver, PA

This dish is full of spring flavors! It's a tasty combination of tender pasta, ham and Swiss cheese, along with spinach, rosemary and a hint of Dijon mustard.

12-oz. pkg. ziti pasta, uncooked
3 T. butter
1/2 c. onion, chopped
1 T. garlic, chopped
10-oz. pkg. frozen chopped
   spinach, thawed and
   well drained
1/4 t. cayenne pepper

1/3 c. all-purpose flour
3 c. 2% milk
2 T. Dijon mustard
3 c. cooked ham, chopped
8-oz. pkg. shredded Swiss
   cheese, divided
1 T. fresh rosemary, chopped
salt and pepper to taste

Cook pasta according to package directions; drain. Meanwhile, in a large saucepan, melt butter over medium heat. Add onion and garlic; sauté until onion is softened, about 5 minutes. Add spinach and cayenne pepper; continue cooking until all liquid is absorbed. Stir in flour and cook for one minute. Stir in milk and mustard; cook until thickened, stirring constantly. Stir in ham, cooked pasta, one cup Swiss cheese and rosemary; mix well until combined. Season with salt and pepper. Transfer to a greased 13"x9" baking pan; top with remaining cheese. Cover and bake at 350 degrees for 30 minutes. Makes 6 servings.

If your favorite casserole tends to bubble over in the oven, place a sheet of aluminum foil under the pan to catch drippings...clean-up's a snap!

Sunday Dinners with Family

Cheese-Stuffed Peppers

Linda Pepple
Buckhannon, WV

Whenever we were at Grandma's on Sunday, this recipe is what she prepared...she knew I loved it. A simple salad is all you need with it. I use fresh-baked cheese bread, which is white bread with shredded Cheddar cheese kneaded in and baked. If you can't find cheese bread, substitute fresh white bread and add some extra Cheddar cheese.

6 green peppers, halved and
    seeds removed
2 T. butter
1 onion, chopped
16-oz. loaf cheese bread,
    torn into chunks

8-oz. pkg. shredded sharp
    Cheddar cheese
1/2 t. pepper
4 c. tomato juice

Arrange green peppers in a greased 13"x9" baking pan; set aside. Melt butter in a skillet over medium heat. Add onion; sauté until softened and golden. In a large bowl, combine bread chunks, onion mixture, cheese, pepper and enough tomato juice to make everything hold together. Mix well with your hands. Fill pepper halves with bread mixture; pour remaining tomato juice over and around peppers. Bake, uncovered, at 350 degrees for 45 minutes. If tops of the peppers are not browned enough, place under the broiler for a few minutes. Makes 6 servings.

Laughter really is the best medicine! Studies show that time spent laughing provides all kinds of health benefits...it may even burn extra calories. So be sure to share funny stories and the kids' latest jokes everyday over dinner.

Mom's Best
Sunday Suppers

Scrumptious Saucy Spareribs

Janis Parr
Ontario, Canada

This is honestly the best recipe for ribs I've ever found. I've made these ribs dozens of times at the request of my family & friends. The sauce is the perfect balance between sweet and savory...and it couldn't be simpler to make!

3 lbs. lean pork side ribs, cut into
   serving-size pieces
1 c. catsup
1/2 c. brown sugar, packed

1/2 c. white vinegar
2-1/4 t. ground ginger
1-1/4 t. garlic powder
1 t. dry mustard

Place ribs in a lightly greased large roasting pan. Cover and bake at 350 degrees for one hour. Remove from oven; drain. Meanwhile, combine remaining ingredients in a bowl; stir well to blend. Taste for sweetness and spiciness, adding more sugar and spice as preferred. Spoon half of sauce mixture over baked ribs; cover and return to oven. Cover and bake for one more hour, checking for tenderness. If ribs are very tender, cover with remaining sauce and serve hot. If ribs aren't yet tender, reserve remaining sauce, replace lid and return to oven until done. When ribs are fully cooked, cover with remaining sauce and serve immediately. Serves 6 to 8.

When the weather is nice, carry dinner to the backyard
for a picnic. You'll be making memories together...and just
about everything seems to taste even better outdoors!

Sunday Dinners with Family

Baked Ham with Balsamic Brown Sugar Glaze

Lynn Williams
Muncie, IN

Baked ham was always on the menu for family dinners at Mom's, especially on Easter Sunday and other holidays. We never tired of it... and we knew there would be yummy ham sandwiches on Monday! Sadly, I never got her recipe, but I like this one almost as well.

6 to 7-lb. fully cooked bone-in
    ham
1 c. brown sugar, packed

2 T. balsamic vinegar
1/2 t. dry mustard

Place ham on a wire rack in a shallow roasting pan, fat-side up. Cover loosely with aluminum foil. Bake at 325 degrees for one hour and 15 minutes to 2 hours and 15 minutes, depending on size of ham. About 20 minutes before ham is done, remove from oven. Pour off drippings from pan; remove skin from ham, if desired. Mix remaining ingredients in a bowl; spoon onto ham. Bake, uncovered, for another 20 minutes, or until a meat thermometer inserted in the thickest part of ham reads 140 degrees. Cover ham to keep warm; let stand about 10 minutes. Slice and serve. Makes 10 to 12 servings.

What is a family, after all, except memories? Haphazard and precious as the contents of a catch-all drawer in the kitchen.

–Joyce Carol Oates

Mom's Best
Sunday Suppers

Pineapple Chicken

Cynthia Robinson
Williston Park, NY

This recipe is a favorite in my family. Everyone goes back for seconds!

4 chicken breasts, cut in half
1/2 c. all-purpose flour
1/3 c. oil
1 t. salt
1/4 t. pepper
20-oz. can pineapple rings,
  drained and juice reserved
1 c. sugar

2 T. cornstarch
3/4 c. cider vinegar
1 T. soy sauce
1/4 t. ground ginger
1 cube chicken bouillon
1 green pepper, cut crosswise
  into 1/4-inch rings
cooked rice

Pat chicken breasts dry with paper towels; coat with flour. Heat oil in a large skillet over medium heat. Add chicken, a few pieces at a time; brown on both sides. Arrange chicken in a lightly greased shallow roasting pan, skin-side up. Season with salt and pepper; set aside. To make sauce, add reserved pineapple juice to a measuring cup; add enough water to equal 1-1/4 cups liquid and pour into a saucepan. Add sugar, cornstarch, vinegar, soy sauce, ginger and bouillon cube. Bring to a boil, stirring constantly. Boil for 2 minutes; spoon over chicken in pan. Bake, uncovered, at 350 degrees for 30 minutes. Top chicken with pineapple and green pepper rings. Bake another 30 minutes, or until chicken is tender. Serve chicken and sauce with cooked rice. Makes 4 servings.

To keep rice from becoming sticky, don't stir it after cooking.
Instead, gently fluff it with a fork. It works every time!

Sunday Dinners with Family

Pam's Oven-Baked Chicken

Pam Hooley
LaGrange, IN

I found this recipe years ago and changed a few ingredients to suit our taste. It's delicious! Serve with a fresh salad, or pop a pan of veggies into the oven to roast along with the chicken.

1 T. butter
1/3 c. biscuit baking mix
1/3 c. cornmeal
1 t. paprika
1/4 t. garlic powder

1-1/2 t. seasoned salt
1/4 t. pepper
3-lb. chicken, cut up, or
    5 chicken thighs or breasts

Add butter to a 13"x9" baking pan; set in 425-degree oven to melt. Meanwhile, mix together baking mix, cornmeal and seasonings in a plastic zipping bag. Add chicken to bag, a few pieces at a time; shake until coated. Arrange chicken in hot pan, skin-side down. Bake, uncovered, at 425 degrees for 35 minutes; turn over. Bake another 10 to 15 minutes, until no longer pink in center. Serves 5.

Money's Worth Meatloaf

Derek Morris
Winston-Salem, NC

My mother used to make this meatloaf often when I was growing up, and it was always one of my favorites. Thankfully, my sister-in-law Pauline has kept the recipe in the family and makes it on special occasions.

1-1/2 lbs. ground beef chuck
1/2 c. soft bread crumbs
2 eggs, beaten
0.6-oz. pkg. Italian salad
    dressing mix
1/2 c. boiling water

2 c. herb-seasoned stuffing
1/2 c. mayonnaise
1/2 c. celery with leaves, chopped
1 t. curry powder
1/2 c. apricot jam, melted

Combine beef, bread crumbs, eggs and dressing mix. Press mixture into a 10-inch by 8-inch rectangle; set aside. Combine boiling water, stuffing, mayonnaise, celery and curry powder; mix well. Spoon in a strip down center of beef; ease beef mixture over stuffing and seal edges. Place seam-side down in an aluminum foil-covered 13"x9" baking pan; chill for one hour. Bake, uncovered, at 350 degrees for 40 minutes, basting several times with melted jam. Slice and serve. Serves 6 to 8.

Baked Penne with Ham, Peas & Jack Cheese

Marcia Shaffer
Conneaut Lake, PA

This is a great recipe and my family loves it. After Easter, I cut up any leftover ham into supper portions, small pieces for use in recipes and, of course, the bone with some meat on it for bean soup. I freeze it for another day when we are hungry for ham again. Some of it I'll use in this easy, filling pasta to serve with a side salad. Pepper Jack cheese gives it a nice pop!

16-oz. pkg. penne pasta,
    uncooked
3 T. olive oil
1/2 c. onion, finely chopped
1 c. tomato, finely chopped
3 T. all-purpose flour
4 c. milk

salt and pepper to taste
8-oz. pkg. shredded Monterey
    Jack cheese, divided
10-oz. pkg. frozen baby peas,
    thawed
1/2 lb. cooked ham, diced

Cook pasta according to package directions; drain and transfer to a large bowl. Meanwhile, in a heavy saucepan, heat oil over medium heat. Add onion and tomato; cook and stir for 2 minutes. Sprinkle with flour; cook and stir for one more minute. Gradually add milk, whisking rapidly until a smooth sauce forms. Season with salt and pepper. Add one cup cheese; cook and stir until melted and smooth. To cooked pasta, add cheese sauce, peas and ham; toss until well blended. Transfer to a greased 3-quart casserole dish; top with remaining cheese. Bake, uncovered, at 350 degrees for about 30 minutes, until bubbly and golden. Serves 6 to 8.

Try adding a chicken bouillon cube to the water when cooking pasta, rice or vegetables. You'll be surprised how much flavor it adds!

Sunday Dinners with Family

Stuffed Pork Loin

Bev Traxler
British Columbia, Canada

This is our special Easter Sunday meal. You can add or substitute ingredients...celery and onion for apples, walnuts for pecans, or simply add an onion soup mix. Great with mashed potatoes, gravy and buttered green beans...a savory, tasty dinner indeed.

4-lb. center-cut pork loin,
   butterflied
6-oz. pkg. chicken stuffing mix
3/4 c. boiling water

1 apple, cored and finely chopped
3/4 c. chopped pecans
3 T. raisins

If the pork loin wasn't purchased already butterflied, place it on a cutting board; use a long, sharp knife to slice lengthwise down the center, leaving about 1/2-inch uncut. Set aside. In a large bowl, combine stuffing mix and boiling water; stir until moistened. Cover and let stand for 5 minutes. Add apple, pecans and raisins; mix lightly. Open and flatten pork loin; spread with stuffing mixture. Roll up pork loin, starting on one long side. Tie roll in several places with kitchen string. Place roll seam-side down on an aluminum foil-covered rimmed baking sheet, lightly sprayed with non-stick vegetable spray. Bake, uncovered, at 400 degrees for 50 minutes to one hour, until a meat thermometer reads 145 degrees. Remove from oven; loosely cover with foil. Let stand for 10 minutes, or to medium doneness of 160 degrees; slice and serve. Makes 12 to 16 servings.

Keep a stash of aprons in big and little sizes for everyone who wants to help out in the kitchen!

Mom's Best
Sunday Suppers

My Own Country Steak

Marcia Shaffer
Conneaut Lake, PA

This recipe tastes so good at a Sunday dinner after church. It's easy to prepare...serve with mashed potatoes to enjoy the gravy.

1 c. all-purpose flour
1 t. seasoned meat tenderizer
1/4 t. pepper
1 lb. beef round steak, cut into
    serving-size pieces

oil for deep frying
10-3/4 oz. can cream of
    mushroom soup
1 c. water
1-1-/2 c. onions, sliced

In a shallow dish, combine flour, tenderizer and pepper; dredge steak pieces in mixture. Heat one inch of oil in a heavy skillet over medium heat. Add steak; cook until browned on both sides. Remove steak to a plate; pour off oil from skillet. Add soup, water and onions to skillet; stir to blend. Return steak to skillet. Cover and simmer over low heat for one hour, or until steak is tender, adding more water as needed. May also bake at 350 degrees for one hour. Serves 4.

Great-Aunt's Oven Stroganoff

Cindy Neel
Gooseberry Patch

This recipe came from my Great-Aunt Sallee. We always enjoyed her cooking at family reunions.

1-1/2 lbs. stew beef cubes
10-3/4 oz. can French onion
    soup
10-3/4 oz. can cream of
    mushroom soup

4-1/2 oz. jar sliced mushrooms,
    drained
cooked egg noodles

Combine all ingredients except noodles in a bowl; mix well. Spread evenly in a greased 3-quart casserole dish. Cover and bake at 350 degrees for 3 hours, stirring occasionally; add a little water, if needed. Serve over cooked noodles. Serves 4 to 6.

For the best results when browning chicken, stew beef or pork chops, pat it dry first, and add to the skillet in batches.

Sunday Dinners with Family

Bacon-Sour Cream Beef Fillets

Sonia Daily
Rochester, MI

Easy yet elegant and delicious...a special-occasion meal. I adapted this from my mother-in-law's recipe and it is my son's favorite "Welcome Home" dish. He made a point of learning how to make it himself and makes it often for his wife and her family. Save money on the steaks by buying a whole beef tenderloin, having it cut into steaks and freezing what you don't need for later.

6 6-oz. beef fillet steaks
salt and pepper to taste
1/2 c. butter
6 slices bacon, chopped

8-oz. pkg. sliced mushrooms
1 c. white wine or beef broth
1 c. sour cream

Season fillets with salt and pepper; set aside. Melt butter in a large skillet over medium-high heat. Add bacon and sauté until crisp. Add fillets; cook until browned on both sides. Remove fillets to a lightly greased 13"x9" baking pan; set aside. Add mushrooms and wine or broth to skillet; simmer for 10 minutes. Spoon mushroom mixture over fillets; allow to cool slightly. Top each fillet with a dollop of sour cream. Bake, uncovered, at 350 degrees for 20 to 30 minutes for medium-rare. Serves 6.

For an extra-special dinner, tuck a small flower or two into dainty egg cups...place one at each table setting.

Mom's Best
Sunday Suppers

Lasagne alla Genovese

Jayne Lipke
Milwaukee, WI

This recipe from my mom was my favorite as a child. I first made it myself when I was dating my husband. He likes to tell people this is why he married me!

9 lasagna noodles, uncooked
3/4 lb. sliced mozzarella cheese, divided

1-1/2 c. dry cottage cheese or ricotta cheese, divided
1/2 c. grated Parmesan cheese

Prepare Meat Sauce ahead of time. Cook noodles according to package directions; drain. In a lightly greased 13"x9" baking pan, layer 1/3 of meat sauce, 1/3 of lasagna noodles, half of mozzarella cheese, half of cottage or ricotta cheese and all of Parmesan cheese. Repeat layering, ending with a layer of noodles and remaining meat sauce on top. Cover and bake at 350 degrees for 45 minutes, or until hot and bubbly. Serves 6.

Meat Sauce:

2 T. olive oil
1 lb. ground beef round
1/2 c. onion, chopped
28-oz. can diced tomatoes
6-oz. can tomato paste
2 T. grated Parmesan cheese
1 T. dried parsley

2 cloves garlic, minced
1 t. dried oregano
1/2 t. dried basil
1/4 t. anise seed
1/2 t. salt
1/4 t. pepper

Heat olive oil in a large skillet over medium heat. Cook beef and onion until beef is browned, breaking up beef; drain. Stir in remaining ingredients. Reduce heat to low. Simmer, uncovered, about 1-1/2 hours, stirring occasionally.

Be sure to have containers on hand to send everyone home with leftovers... if there are any!

Sunday Dinners with Family

Bus Grandmom's Meatloaf

Carol Barnes
East Greenville, PA

This meatloaf has been in my family for many, many years and was always a favorite at Sunday dinners! We call it by a sentimental name given to my grandmother who always rode the bus...thus, Bus Grandmom! (The other grandmother always arrived in a camper, so she was Camper Grandmom.) Grandmom has long since passed, but her recipe is still loved by all of us.

1-1/2 lbs. ground beef
1 c. rolled oats, uncooked
1/2 c. celery, chopped
1/2 c. onion, chopped
1 T. dried parsley
1/2 t. dry mustard

Optional: salt to taste
1 egg, lightly beaten
1/4 c. milk
1 T. Worcestershire sauce
1/4 c. catsup

In a large bowl, combine beef, oats, celery, onion, parsley, mustard and salt, if desired. Mix well and set aside. In a separate bowl, whisk together egg, milk and Worcestershire sauce. Add egg mixture to beef mixture and combine well. Turn into a greased 11"x8" baking pan, patting into a loaf shape. Bake, uncovered, at 350 degrees for 45 minutes. Top with catsup; return to oven for an additional 5 minutes. Slice and serve. Makes 6 servings.

Cut leftover meatloaf into thick slices, wrap individually and freeze. Later, they can be thawed and rewarmed quickly for scrumptious meatloaf sandwiches at a few moments' notice.

Mom's Best
Sunday Suppers

Red Beans & Rice Casserole
Pam Lunn
Pensacola, FL

My husband, who was born and raised in Louisiana, loves the classic red beans & rice. But I don't always have the time to cook a pot of beans. This easy and delicious recipe comes together in a snap, and has my Cajun husband's approval. I like to serve it with homemade cornbread on the side.

1 c. long-cooking rice, uncooked
6 T. butter, divided
1 bunch green onions, chopped
3 stalks celery, chopped
3/4 c. green pepper, chopped
1 t. garlic, chopped

14-oz. pkg. smoked pork
  sausage link, sliced
2 15-1/2 oz. cans red beans,
  drained and rinsed
Creole seasoning to taste
14-1/2 oz. can chicken broth

Cook rice according to package directions. Meanwhile, melt 4 tablespoons butter in a large non-stick skillet; add onions, celery and green pepper. Sauté for about 10 minutes, until softened and translucent. Add garlic; sauté for one minute. Remove vegetables from skillet; set aside. In the same skillet, melt remaining butter; add sausage and cook until lightly browned on both sides. Return vegetables to skillet; add beans and cooked rice. Season with Creole seasoning and stir to combine. Spoon mixture into a 13"x9" baking pan coated with non-stick vegetable spray; pour chicken broth over all. Bake, uncovered, at 350 degrees for 25 minutes, or until heated through. Serves 6 to 8.

Set out a guest book when friends come to Sunday dinner.
Ask everyone young and old to sign...it will become
a treasured memento.

Sunday Dinners with Family

Smothered Pork Chops

Nancy McCann
Largo, FL

This recipe makes a heart-healthy meal that's tasty enough for Sunday dinner. Serve with your favorite steamed vegetable.

1 onion, chopped
3 to 4 cloves garlic, pressed
6 pork chops, 3/4-inch thick
1/2 c. water

1/3 c. all-purpose flour
14-1/2 oz. can fat-free chicken
    broth
1 T. browning & seasoning sauce

Coat a large skillet with non-stick vegetable spray. Add onion and garlic; sauté over medium heat until tender. Add pork chops and brown on both sides. Add water; bring to a boil. In a bowl, whisk together flour, chicken broth and browning sauce until smooth. Add to skillet, stirring well. Cover and simmer over low heat for 30 to 40 minutes, until pork chops are tender. Makes 6 servings.

Try Mom's secret for the most delicious mashed potatoes... mayonnaise! A big dollop of mayonnaise added while mashing the potatoes adds flavor and creaminess.

Mom's Best
Sunday Suppers

Comfort Chicken

Leona Krivda
Belle Vernon, PA

I have been making this recipe for years and my whole family likes it. It is quick, easy and great for company.

8 boneless, skinless chicken breasts
garlic powder, salt and pepper to taste
8 slices Swiss cheese
2 10-3/4 oz. cans cream of chicken soup
1-1/4 c. white wine or chicken broth
6-oz. pkg. chicken-flavored stuffing mix
1/2 c. butter, melted

Arrange chicken in a single layer in a greased 13"x9" baking pan; sprinkle lightly with seasonings. Top each piece of chicken with a slice of cheese; set aside. In a bowl, whisk together chicken soup and wine or broth; spoon over chicken. Sprinkle with seasoning from stuffing mix. Crush stuffing pieces smaller and put on top to cover well. Drizzle melted butter over all. Bake, uncovered, at 350 degrees for one hour and 15 minutes, or until chicken juices run clear when pierced. Makes 8 servings.

Fresh Salad Dressing
½ cup olive oil
⅓ cup fresh lemon juice
1 Tab. Dijon Mustard
Salt & Pepper to taste
SHAKE!

A simple green salad goes well with all kinds of delicious main dishes. For a zippy lemon dressing, shake up 1/2 cup olive oil, 1/3 cup fresh lemon juice and a tablespoon of Dijon mustard in a small jar and chill to blend.

Sunday Dinners with Family

Mom's Chicken Delight

Shirley Howie
Foxboro, MA

Mom made this chicken often, as it was so quick & easy to put together and we all really liked it! Now I make it for my hubby and me, and it always comes out tender and juicy. Mashed potatoes make a perfect side dish. Yum!

5 chicken breasts or thighs
1/2 c. catsup
1/4 c. water

1/4 c. brown sugar, packed
1-oz. pkg. onion soup mix

Arrange chicken in a single layer in a lightly greased 13"x9" baking pan; set aside. In a bowl, whisk together remaining ingredients. Spoon over chicken, making sure that each piece is evenly coated. Cover and bake at 350 degrees for one to 1-1/2 hours, until chicken is tender and juices run clear when pierced. Makes 5 servings.

Mom's Tender Cube Steak

Debbie Adkins
Nicholasville, KY

Growing up in the 50s and 60s, cube steak was one of my favorites that my mom made in a pressure cooker. Nowadays, it's so easy to fix in an electric pressure cooker. No matter how tough the steak might be, this method will make it super tender!

1 c. all-purpose flour
3/4 t. salt
1 t. pepper
4 6-oz. beef cube steaks

2 to 3 t. oil
1-1/2 c. beef broth
1/2 c. water

Whisk together flour, salt and pepper in a shallow dish. Dredge steaks in flour mixture. Add oil to a large skillet; heat over medium-high heat until very hot. Brown steaks on both sides; drain and place in an electric pressure cooker. Add beef broth and water. Secure lid; set pressure release to Sealing. Cook on Meat setting for 20 to 25 minutes. Use natural release; open carefully and serve. Makes 4 servings.

Mom's Best
Sunday Suppers

Mini Chicken Pot Pies

Debbie Benzi
Binghamton, NY

My family loves chicken pot pie, and this version is their favorite. It's fun to make and serve on a chilly Sunday afternoon. This may also be prepared in a 13x9 inch baking pan; bake until hot and bubbly, about 30 to 40 minutes.

6 T. butter
2 lbs. boneless, skinless chicken
   breasts, cubed
3 t. kosher salt, divided
1 t. pepper, divided
2 c. potatoes, peeled and chopped
1-1/2 c. carrots, peeled and
   chopped
1-1/2 c. celery, sliced
1/2 c. onion, chopped

3 cloves garlic, minced
3/4 c. all-purpose flour
1/2 c. dry white wine or water
4-1/2 c. chicken broth
1 T. dried thyme
1 c. sour cream
1 sheet frozen puff pastry,
   thawed
1 egg, lightly beaten

In a large Dutch oven, melt butter over medium heat. Season chicken with one teaspoon salt and 1/2 teaspoon pepper; add to pan and cook for 3 minutes. Add vegetables and garlic to pan. Cook until tender, about 10 minutes, stirring occasionally. Sprinkle with flour and remaining salt and pepper. Cook, stirring constantly, for 2 minutes. Add wine or water; cook for 2 minutes. Add broth and thyme; bring to a boil. Reduce heat to medium-low and simmer until thickened, about 8 minutes. Stir in sour cream. Divide chicken mixture among 8 to 10 individual casserole dishes. On a lightly floured surface, roll out puff pastry sheet. Cut pastry into 8 to 10 circles, using a plate slightly larger than the diameter of dishes as a guide. Top each dish with a pastry circle, crimping edges to seal. Cut several slits with a knife tip; brush with beaten egg. Bake at 400 degrees for about 25 minutes, until pastry is golden and filling is hot and bubbly. Serves 8 to 10.

Cut vents in pot pie crusts with
a chicken-shaped mini
cookie cutter...so sweet.

Casual Sunday Suppers

Fiesta Chicken Bake

Beckie Apple
Grannis, AR

I've been making this easy chicken bake for years and we never get tired of it! It goes together in a snap. While it's baking, I have time to fix a chopped salad to serve alongside it.

10-3/4 oz. can cream of
    mushroom soup
10-3/4 oz. can chicken
    noodle soup
10-oz. can diced tomatoes with
    mild green chiles
4-oz. can sliced mushrooms

12-1/2 oz. can chunk chicken
    breast, drained and broth
    reserved
11-oz. pkg. nacho cheese tortilla
    chips, divided
8-oz. pkg. shredded Cheddar
    cheese, divided

In a large bowl, combine soups, tomatoes with juice, mushrooms with juice and reserved broth from canned chicken. Mix until well blended. Flake chicken with a fork and add to soup mixture; stir to combine. In a lightly greased 13"x9" baking pan, layer half each of tortilla chips, cheese and soup mixture. Repeat layering. Bake, uncovered, at 325 degrees for 25 to 30 minutes, until bubbly and golden. Makes 4 to 6 servings.

Prefer to shred your own cheese? Place the wrapped cheese in the freezer for 10 to 20 minutes...it will just glide across the grater.

Casual Sunday Suppers

Mom's Bacon Spaghetti

Laura Esposito
Nesconset, NY

My mom made this often for us growing up, and we all agreed that nothing smells better than bacon and onions! Recently we changed the recipe a little, and we think it's even easier and more delicious now.

16-oz. pkg. spaghetti, uncooked
1/2 lb. bacon, chopped
3/4 c. onion, diced
1 clove garlic, pressed
2 T. tomato paste
14-1/2 oz. can tomato sauce

14-1/2 oz. can petite diced
   tomatoes
pepper to taste
2/3 c. grated Pecorino Romano
   cheese

Cook spaghetti according to package directions; drain. Transfer spaghetti to a large serving bowl; cover to keep warm. Meanwhile, in a skillet over medium heat, cook bacon until crisp. Remove bacon to a paper towel-lined plate and set aside. Drain skillet, reserving 3 tablespoons drippings in skillet. Cook onion in drippings until softened and translucent. Add garlic; cook for one minute. Stir in tomato paste; cook for another minute. Stir in tomato sauce, tomatoes with juice and pepper. Reduce heat to medium-low; simmer for 10 minutes, or until slightly thickened. Add sauce and cheese to spaghetti in bowl; mix well and serve. Makes 4 to 6 servings.

Make a warm loaf of crostini for dinner...a tasty go-with for pasta. Slice a loaf of Italian bread into 1/2-inch slices. Brush olive oil over both sides of each slice; sprinkle with coarse salt. Bake at 300 degrees for 20 minutes, or until toasty, turning once.

Tuna Melt Panini

Nancy Kailihiwa
Wheatland, CA

I watched my dad make all kinds of unique sandwiches when I was growing up. So I came up with this one in his honor...it was a big hit! It's fun to serve it in a deli-style basket with classic potato chips and carrot sticks, just like Dad would do.

2 12-oz cans chunk light tuna,
    drained and flaked
4 to 6 T. mayonnaise
2 T. sweet pickle relish
1 T. mustard
4 to 8 shakes hot pepper sauce

Optional: 1 t. salt
1/2 t. pepper
8 slices hearty whole-grain bread
1/4 c. butter, softened
8 slices Pepper Jack cheese

In a bowl, combine all ingredients except bread, butter and cheese; mix well and set aside. Spread one side of each bread slice with 1/2 tablespoon butter. Heat a panini maker on medium setting. Place one slice of bread butter-side down on panini grill. Top with a slice of cheese; add 1/4 of tuna mixture and spread over bread, leaving a small gap around the edge. Top with another slice of cheese and another slice of bread, butter-side up. Close panini maker. Cook until bread is grilled and cheese is melted, about 4 to 6 minutes. Serve immediately. Makes 4 sandwiches.

Stir up a scrumptious dill sauce for salmon or tuna. Blend 1/2 cup sour cream, one tablespoon Dijon mustard, one tablespoon lemon juice and 2 teaspoons chopped fresh dill. Chill before serving.

Casual Sunday Suppers

Diner-Style Chicken-Fried Burgers

Lynda Hart
Bluffdale, UT

This is a quick dinner favorite. Serve piping-hot with mashed potatoes and steamed vegetables.

1 lb. ground beef
1/2 c. onion, finely chopped
1/4 c. milk
1/2 c. all-purpose flour
1/2 t. garlic powder
salt and pepper to taste
1 egg, beaten
20 round buttery crackers, crushed
4 t. oil

In a large bowl, combine beef and onion; mix well and form into 5 to 6 patties. Set up coatings in 4 shallow bowls: milk in the first, flour with seasonings in the second, beaten egg in the third, and crushed crackers in the last bowl. Dip each patty into milk, flour mixture, egg and crackers, coating well. Heat oil in a skillet over medium-high heat. Reduce heat to low; add patties and cook on both sides until browned and beef is cooked through. Makes 5 to 6 servings.

Welcome a new bride into the family with copies of her new hubby's best childhood photos. Add amusing and heartfelt captions and tuck into a small photo album. Remember to add a few of his favorite recipes!

Mom's Best
Sunday Suppers

Jalapeño Popper Skillet Dinner
Sonja Meyer
Harper, TX

I had so many jalapeños in my garden one year that I was having a hard time coming up with ways to use them. My family loves jalapeño poppers, so I came up with this easy and fun skillet dinner. It was a hit! Serve with a green salad. Enjoy!

16-oz. pkg. penne pasta,
  uncooked
8 boneless, skinless chicken
  thighs, cut into bite-size
  pieces
salt and pepper to taste
2 to 4 t. oil

1 lb. bacon, cut into bite-size
  pieces
20 jalapeño peppers, halved and
  seeds removed
8-oz. pkg. cream cheese,
  softened
2 c. half-and-half

Cook pasta according to package directions; drain. Meanwhile, season chicken with salt and pepper. Heat oil in a large deep skillet over medium heat. Add chicken to skillet; cook until nearly done. Add bacon to skillet; continue cooking until chicken and bacon are done. Add jalapeños to skillet; cook until soft. Add cream cheese; stir until melted. Add half-and-half; stir until a creamy sauce forms. Add cooked pasta to skillet; stir well and serve. Serves 8.

Hosting a cookout for family & friends? Serve nostalgic soft drinks like root beer, orange pop and grape fizz in glass bottles, just for fun!

Casual Sunday Suppers

Easy Sausage Cassoulet

Melanie Springer
Canton, OH

This is a great, hearty dinner for a chilly Sunday evening. I just add a tossed salad and some warm rolls...everyone is happy!

1 lb. Italian pork sausage links,
    casing removed
3/4 c. onion, thinly sliced
2 carrots, peeled and thinly sliced
15-1/2 oz. can Great Northern
    beans
15-1/2 oz. can kidney beans,
    drained and rinsed
1 t. dried thyme
1 t. dried marjoram
salt and pepper to taste
Garnish: chopped fresh parsley

Coat a large skillet with non-stick vegetable spray; heat over medium heat. Break up sausage and add to skillet. Cook sausage about 15 minutes, stirring occasionally, until browned. Remove sausage to a bowl; drain most of the drippings from skillet. Add onion and carrots to skillet; cook 5 to 7 minutes, until onion is tender. Add Great Northern beans, drained kidney beans and seasonings; mix well. Return sausage to skillet, placing on top of vegetables. Cover and cook over medium-low heat for 12 to 15 minutes. Stir well; top with parsley and serve. Makes 4 to 6 servings.

Use your garden's bounty to create a colorful, casual centerpiece. Squash, peppers, eggplant, onions and shallots are beautiful piled in baskets and country containers. Later, use the vegetables in soups and casseroles...add onions and shallots to stews and sauces for flavor.

Mom's Best
Sunday Suppers

Pizza Chicken

Denise Herr
West Jefferson, OH

This recipe can be adapted to other delicious combinations by just changing the toppings. The possibilities are endless...and it's so good! Serve chicken with a crisp salad or spooned over pasta.

2 T. olive oil
4 boneless, skinless chicken
  breasts
4 t. Italian or pizza seasoning
salt and pepper to taste
1 c. marinara sauce
1 c. shredded mozzarella or
  provolone cheese

Optional: browned and
  crumbled Italian sausage,
  chopped pepperoni, sliced
  pepperoncini peppers,
  tomatoes, black olives,
  mushrooms

Heat oil in a large skillet over medium heat. Sprinkle chicken with seasonings; add chicken to skillet and brown on both sides. Drain; transfer chicken to a greased 13"x9" baking pan. Top chicken evenly with sauce, cheese and desired toppings. Bake, uncovered, at 350 degrees for 20 minutes, or until chicken juices run clear. Makes 4 servings.

Taco Chicken variation:

2 T. olive oil
4 boneless, skinless chicken
  breasts
4 t. taco seasoning mix
1 c. favorite salsa
1 c. shredded Monterey
  Jack cheese

Optional: browned taco beef and
  chopped green chiles
Garnish: green onions, tomatoes,
  pico de gallo, shredded
  lettuce, sour cream, chopped
  fresh cilantro, crushed tortilla
  chips

Prepare as above, adding salsa, cheese, taco beef and chiles before baking, as desired. Add desired toppings; serve with rice and beans.

Now and then, it's good to pause in our pursuit of happiness and just be happy.
–Guillaume Apollinaire

46

Casual Sunday Suppers

Mexican Lasagna

Valerie Jackson
Salem, UT

This is a quick & easy dinner to toss together that my whole family loves. I always have the ingredients on hand. Top with sour cream, salsa, guacamole or any other toppings your family likes.

1 lb. ground beef
24-oz. jar favorite salsa
16-oz. can refried beans
6 8-inch flour tortillas

16-oz. pkg. shredded Cheddar or
    Monterey Jack cheese, or a
    combo, divided

Brown beef in a skillet over medium heat; drain. Stir in salsa and refried beans. In a greased 13"x9" baking pan, layer 2 flour tortillas; top with half of beef mixture and 1/3 of the cheese. Repeat layers. Top with remaining tortillas and cheese. Cover with aluminum foil, if desired. Bake at 350 degrees for 30 to 40 minutes, until hot and bubbly. Cut into squares to serve. Makes 6 servings.

Cheesy Chicken Enchiladas

Rita Morgan
Pueblo, CO

This is an easy supper dish, made with leftover chicken from another meal. Use your favorite green or red salsa.

16-oz. jar favorite salsa, divided
1-1/2 c. cooked chicken,
    shredded
1/2 c. sour cream

1-1/2 c. shredded Cheddar Jack
    cheese, divided
8 6-inch corn or flour tortillas,
    warmed

Spread 1/2 cup salsa in a lightly greased 11"x8" baking pan; set aside. In a bowl, combine 1/4 cup salsa, chicken, sour cream and 1/2 cup cheese. Spoon 3 tablespoons chicken mixture down the center of each tortilla. Roll up tortillas; place seam-side down in pan. Top with remaining salsa. Bake, uncovered, at 375 degrees for 15 minutes. Top with remaining cheese. Bake for another 5 minutes, or until cheese is melted. Makes 4 servings.

Mom's Best
Sunday Suppers

Brian's Enchi-Lasagna

Louise Graybiel
Ontario, Canada

This is my husband Brian's favorite meal, so don't tell him how easy it is to make! It's a great way to use up leftover meat and rice.

1/4 c. cooked chicken, turkey, beef or pork, diced or shredded
1/2 c. cooked rice
1 t. chili powder
10-3/4 oz. can tomato soup
1/4 c. chunky salsa
4 10-inch flour tortillas, cut into quarters
16-oz. can refried beans
1 c. shredded Monterey Jack cheese

In a bowl, combine meat, rice and chili powder; mix well and set aside. In a separate bowl, mix soup and salsa. Line the bottom of a greased 9"x9" baking pan with 4 overlapping tortilla quarters to cover the bottom. Spoon beans over tortillas; smooth with the back of the spoon to make an even layer. Top with 4 overlapping tortilla quarters to cover. Add meat mixture; smooth evenly. Top with 4 more tortilla quarters. Spoon soup mixture over top; shake pan slightly so mixture runs down into lower layers. Top with last 4 tortilla quarters; sprinkle with cheese. Bake, uncovered, at 350 degrees for 40 minutes, or until bubbly and golden. Serves 4.

Use Mom's vintage casserole dishes to serve up favorite recipes with sweet memories. If you don't have any of hers, keep an eye open at tag sales and thrift stores...you may find the very same kind of dishes she used!

Casual Sunday Suppers

Mom's Stroganoff Loaf

Georgia Muth
Penn Valley, CA

When I found this recipe in my mom's recipe box, it brought back childhood memories of comfort food. It can be served as a main meal, cut into larger slices, or as an appetizer, cut into smaller slices.

1-1/2 lbs. ground beef
1/2 c. onion, chopped
1 c. water
1/2 c. sour cream
1-1/2 oz. pkg. beef stroganoff
   mix

1/4 c. sliced black olives, drained
1 large loaf French bread,
   halved lengthwise
1/4 c. butter, softened
1 c. shredded Cheddar cheese

Brown beef with onion in a skillet over medium heat; drain. Add water, sour cream, stroganoff mix and olives; stir well. Meanwhile, spread cut sides of loaf with butter. Place on a baking sheet and bake at 375 degrees for a few minutes, until lightly toasted. Spread beef mixture on both halves of loaf; top with cheese. Bake, uncovered, at 375 degrees for 8 to 10 minutes. Slice and serve. Makes 12 servings.

Let the kids lend a hand in the kitchen! Preschoolers can wash veggies, fold napkins and set the table. Older children can measure, shred, chop, stir and maybe even help with meal planning and grocery shopping.

Chicken Avocado Burritos

Diana Krol
Hutchinson, KS

My whole family loves these burritos! They're a quick go-to meal when I have some leftover roast chicken. Serve with Mexican rice or a simple salad on the side.

2 c. cooked chicken, shredded
1 c. shredded Colby cheese
1 avocado, peeled, pitted
 and diced
1/2 t. chili powder
Optional: 2 T. fresh cilantro,
 chopped; 1/2 t. ground cumin
4 10-inch flour tortillas
1/4 c. sour cream, divided

1 T. oil
Garnish: shredded lettuce,
 chopped tomatoes, sliced
 green onions, sliced black
 olives, sliced jalapeño
 peppers, sour cream,
 shredded cheese, picante
 sauce

In a large bowl, gently stir together chicken, cheese, avocado, chili powder, cilantro and/or cumin as desired. Spread each tortilla with one tablespoon sour cream; top with 1/4 of chicken mixture. Roll filled tortillas into burritos; secure with wooden toothpicks. Heat oil in a skillet over medium heat. Cook burritos, turning as needed, until golden on all sides. Remove toothpicks and serve, garnished with desired toppings. Serves 4.

Try adding a little cinnamon to Mexican-style dishes. Just a sprinkle goes well alongside chili powder, cumin and other south-of-the-border flavors.

Casual Sunday Suppers

Easy Crescent Pizza Bake

Mel Chencharick
Julian, PA

This is one of the easiest pizzas I've ever tried! You can top with anything you or your family likes. Kids love to help make this!

1 c. ground beef or ground
  pork sausage
1 c. pizza sauce
1/2 c. green pepper, chopped
8-oz. tube refrigerated crescent
  dinner rolls

1 c. shredded mozzarella cheese
25 slices pepperoni
Garnish: fresh basil or oregano,
  snipped

Brown beef or sausage in a skillet over medium heat for 8 to 10 minutes; drain. Stir in pizza sauce and green pepper; simmer for 5 minutes. Meanwhile, separate rolls into 8 triangles. Arrange triangles in an ungreased 9"x9" baking pan or 10" pie plate, pressing into the bottom and up the sides to form a crust. Spoon beef mixture into crust-lined pan. Sprinkle with cheese; top with pepperoni. Bake, uncovered, at 375 degrees for 14 to 17 minutes, until crust is golden and cheese is melted. Top with basil or oregano. Makes 6 servings.

Whip up some pizza sauce in a jiffy...no cooking needed.
In a blender, combine a can of seasoned diced tomatoes,
a little garlic and a shake of Italian seasoning.
Purée to the desired consistency.

Bar-B-Que Burgers

Marsha Nichols
El Reno, OK

Our family loves this! It was my mom's recipe...you may know it as Sloppy Joes. The recipe appeared in our church's cookbook back in the 1960s and we still enjoy it today. Just add some potato chips and a dill pickle for a tasty meal.

1 lb. ground beef
3/4 c. onion, chopped
10-3/4 oz. can tomato soup
1 T. Worcestershire sauce
1 T. vinegar
2 t. chili powder
1 t. sugar
1 t. nutmeg
1 t. cinnamon
salt to taste
8 hamburger buns, split

In a skillet over medium heat, cook beef with onion until browned; drain. Stir in remaining ingredients except buns. Simmer over low heat for 15 minutes, stirring occasionally. To serve, spoon onto warm buns. Makes 8 servings.

A diner-themed meal is fun for the whole family.
Make place mats from vintage maps, roll up flatware
in paper napkins and serve catsup & mustard
from plastic squeeze bottles.

Casual Sunday Suppers

Mexican Pita Pizzas

Blake Toonstra
Grand Rapids, MI

*This is a great meal for family game or movie night...
just add some tortilla chips and salsa!*

6 pita rounds
15-oz. jar pizza sauce
2 to 4 c. shredded Mexican-blend
   cheese
1 onion, diced

2 tomatoes, diced
1 green pepper, thinly sliced
   into rings
Optional: sliced hot peppers
   to taste

Arrange pitas on ungreased baking sheets; top with pizza sauce
and desired amount of cheese. Add remaining ingredients. Bake at
375 degrees for 15 to 20 minutes, until pitas are golden and cheese
is melted. Makes 6 servings.

Sunday Supper Chicken

Teresa Eller
Kansas City, KS

*So easy! Sometimes I pull the chicken off the bone and we have it on
sandwiches, sometimes I serve with a side of baked beans. Save and
freeze the chicken broth for homemade soup or chicken & dumplings.*

8 pieces bone-in, skin-on
   chicken
4 c. water

4 cubes chicken bouillon
2 c. favorite barbecue sauce

Spray a 5-quart slow cooker with non-stick vegetable spray. Layer
chicken in crock; add water and bouillon cubes. Cover and cook on high
setting for 3 to 4 hours, or low setting for 5 to 7 hours, until chicken is
very tender. Drain broth, reserving it for another recipe. Shred chicken,
discarding skin and bones; return to crock and stir in barbecue sauce.
Toss to coat and serve. Serves 4 to 6.

An ounce of mother is worth a pound of clergy.
   –Spanish proverb

Mom's Best
Sunday Suppers

Chicken Cordon Bleu Sandwiches

Karen Ensign
Providence, UT

You'll love this recipe...it's tasty grilled cheese that tastes like Chicken Cordon Bleu! A quick and delicious meal.

2 T. cream cheese, softened
2 T. light mayonnaise
1 t. Dijon mustard
1/4 c. panko bread crumbs
12 slices whole-wheat bread
12 slices bacon, crisply cooked

12 slices deli baked ham
2 cooked chicken breasts, shredded
1 c. shredded mozzarella or Swiss cheese, or 6 slices
1/2 c. butter, softened

In a bowl, blend cream cheese, mayonnaise, mustard and panko crumbs. Spread one tablespoon of mixture over each of 6 slices of bread. Layer with bacon, ham, chicken and mozzarella cheese; top with another slice of bread. Spread butter on outsides of sandwiches. Grill sandwiches on a non-stick skillet or griddle over medium heat until golden. Flip over; grill other side until golden. Serve warm. Makes 6 servings.

Just for fun, spear a cherry tomato or a tiny sweet pickle with a long toothpick and use as a garnish for overstuffed sandwiches.

Casual Sunday Suppers

Any-Day Comfort Casserole

Bev Traxler
British Columbia, Canada

Pure comfort food...great for a busy family, and a snap to prepare.

2 15-oz. cans pork & beans in
  tomato sauce
1 lb. hot dogs or smoked pork
  sausages, cut into one-inch
  pieces
10-3/4 oz. can tomato soup

1 T. Worcestershire sauce
1 t. mustard
1/4 c. brown sugar, packed
1/8 t. nutmeg
5 to 6 apple rings, unpeeled
  and cored

In a large bowl, mix together pork & beans, hot dogs or sausages, tomato soup, Worcestershire sauce and mustard. Turn into a lightly greased 2-quart casserole dish. Bake, uncovered, at 350 degrees for 15 minutes. Meanwhile, in a cup, mix brown sugar and nutmeg. Remove casserole from oven; arrange apple rings on top and sprinkle with brown sugar mixture. Bake an additional 5 minutes, or until apples are tender. Makes 6 to 8 servings.

Make a fresh-tasting side dish. Combine 3 to 4 sliced zucchini, 1/2 teaspoon minced garlic and a tablespoon of chopped fresh basil. Sauté in a little olive oil until tender and serve warm.

Mom's Best
Sunday Suppers

Crustless Green Chile Quiche

Nancy Albers Shore
Midland, GA

A friend shared this recipe with me, and with a few adjustments, we've come up with a favorite breakfast or light supper! I like to serve this with a tossed green salad for an easy lunch or brunch, or with biscuits for a brunch treat.

1 lb. ground beef, browned
  and drained
1/4 t. ground cumin
salt and pepper to taste
4 eggs, lightly beaten
1 c. evaporated milk
2 T. all-purpose flour
4-oz. can chopped green chiles,
  drained

1 c. shredded Monterey Jack or
  Pepper Jack cheese
1/2 c. shredded sharp Cheddar
  cheese
Optional: salsa, sour cream,
  additional cheese

In a large bowl, combine browned beef, cumin, salt and pepper; set aside. In another bowl, stir together eggs, milk, flour, chiles and cheeses. Spoon egg mixture over beef mixture; stir to combine. Transfer mixture to a greased 9" deep-dish glass pie plate or quiche pan. Bake, uncovered, at 400 degrees for 15 minutes. Reduce heat to 325 degrees. Bake for 30 minutes more, or until a knife tip inserted near the center comes out clean. Let stand 5 to 10 minutes; cut into wedges. Garnish as desired and serve. Makes 6 to 8 servings.

Make your own salsa to serve with Crustless Green Chile Quiche. In a blender, combine a 15-ounce can of stewed tomatoes, several slices of canned jalapeños and a teaspoon or 2 of jalapeño juice. Process to the desired consistency.

Casual Sunday Suppers

Layered Mexicali Stack

Charlene Ratzlow
Loves Park, IL

This is an original creation of mine. Yum!

1 lb. ground beef sirloin	3 10-inch flour tortillas
1 pkg. taco seasoning mix	8-oz. pkg. finely shredded
8-oz. jar mild picante sauce	Mexican white cheese
8-oz. jar mild chunky salsa	Garnish: sour cream, guacamole

Brown beef in a skillet over medium heat; drain. Mix in taco seasoning, picante sauce and salsa. In a greased 13"x9" glass baking pan, layer tortillas alternately with beef mixture, ending with beef mixture on top. Cover with non-stick aluminum foil. Bake at 350 degrees for one hour. Top with cheese and bake another 30 minutes, watching carefully to avoid burning. Let stand several minutes; cut into slices and serve, with garnishes set out in bowls. Serves 4.

Is dinner taking a little longer than expected? Just soften an 8-ounce block of cream cheese, set it on a serving plate and spoon salsa over the top. Serve with tortilla chips and crackers.

Mom's Best
Sunday Suppers

Cheeseburger Pizza

Joanna Gall
Edison, OH

Who doesn't love cheeseburgers and pizza? The best thing about this recipe...it's completely kid-friendly! It's easy to make just the way your family likes with traditional burger toppings, too.

1 lb. ground beef
1/4 c. mayonnaise
1/4 c. catsup
2 T. hot pepper sauce
12-inch prebaked Italian
  pizza crust
2 to 3 t. olive oil

8-oz. pkg. shredded Cheddar
  cheese
1/4 c. onion, chopped
1/4 c. pickle, chopped
Garnish: mayonnaise, catsup
  and mustard

Brown beef in a skillet over medium heat; drain and set aside. Mix mayonnaise, catsup and hot sauce in a small bowl; set aside. Preheat grill or oven to 350 degrees. Lightly brush both sides of pizza crust with olive oil; place crust face-down on grill or oven rack for 2 to 3 minutes, until top of crust is golden. Flip crust and brush with mayonnaise mixture; top with beef, shredded cheese, onion and pickle. Grill or bake for 10 to 15 minutes, until cheese is melted. Garnish as desired; cut into wedges. Makes 4 servings.

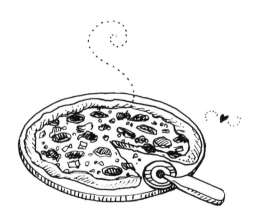

For a crisp pizzeria-style finish, dust the pizza pan
with cornmeal before adding the crust.

Casual Sunday Suppers

Special Grilled Cheese

Liz Plotnick-Snay
Gooseberry Patch

I made so many grilled American cheese sandwiches for my son and his friends when they were young. I've created these special, adult grilled cheese sandwiches for my husband and me.

2 thick or thin slices favorite
   French or hearty grain bread
2 to 3 t. butter, softened
2 to 3 slices white Cheddar or
   Brie cheese

1 ripe pear, cored and
   thinly sliced

Lightly coat one side of each slice of bread with butter. Layer cheese and pear slices on one slice of bread; close sandwich with remaining slice. Heat a skillet over medium heat. Add sandwich; cover (if using Cheddar) and cook until bread is golden and cheese is melted, about 2 minutes per side. Makes one sandwich.

Grilled Cheese Quesadillas

Amy Thomason Hunt
Traphill, NC

These quesadillas are great for a quick supper before going out to game practice or an evening of trick-or-treating. Just add a bowl of tomato soup and presto...happy tummies! A tasty way to use odds & ends of cheese, too.

8 8-inch flour tortillas
1/2 c. shredded Cheddar cheese,
   divided
1/2 c. shredded Pepper Jack
   cheese, divided

1/2 c. shredded mozzarella
   cheese, divided

Spray a skillet with non-stick vegetable spray; heat over medium heat. Add one tortilla to skillet; sprinkle with 2 tablespoons of each cheese and top with another tortilla. Cook until golden and flip. Cook the other side until golden and cheeses are melted. Repeat with remaining tortillas and cheese; cut into quarters to serve. Serves 4.

Mom's Best
Sunday Suppers

Chicken Salad with Dill Pickles

Phyl Broich Wessling
Garner, IA

Here is one of our favorite chicken salad recipes...we love it for an easy Sunday night supper. What makes the difference is the dill pickles. This also makes a great sandwich or pita filling. Simple to keep on hand for a snack anytime.

2 c. cooked chicken breast, shredded
3 medium whole dill pickles, chopped
1/4 c. green onions, chopped
1/2 c. chopped walnuts
1/4 c. slivered or chopped almonds
1/2 to 1 c. mayonnaise, to taste
Garnish: lettuce leaves, cherry tomatoes, fresh parsley

Prepare Poached Chicken ahead of time; cover and chill. In a bowl, combine chicken, pickles, onions and nuts. Stir in mayonnaise; cover and chill. To serve, line 4 salad plates with lettuce leaves; divide chicken salad among plates. Garnish with cherry tomatoes and fresh parsley. Serves 4.

Poached Chicken:

1-1/2 lbs. boneless, skinless chicken breasts
1 onion, quartered
1 cube chicken bouillon
1 T. fresh parsley, chopped
1/4 to 1/2 t. seasoned salt

Combine all ingredients in a large saucepan; add enough water to cover. Bring to a boil; reduce heat to medium-low. Simmer until chicken is tender, about 30 minutes. Remove from heat and cool. Shred chicken; cover and refrigerate.

Save extra chicken broth by freezing in an ice cube tray.
Add the broth cubes when cooking rice or veggies...
a real flavor boost!

Casual Sunday Suppers

Roast Beef Hoagie Pizza

Cyndy Nene
New Castle, PA

This pizza is so easy to make and tastes just like an old-fashioned hoagie. You can change the meat to suit your taste...use any combination of your favorite deli meats, such as ham, salami or turkey. Alongside a salad, it makes a fast, easy dinner.

12-inch prebaked Italian
   pizza crust
1/4 c. mayonnaise
1 lb. sliced deli roast beef
1 onion, thinly sliced

8-oz. pkg. shredded mozzarella
   or provolone cheese
1 c. lettuce, shredded
1 tomato, thinly sliced

Place pizza crust on an ungreased baking sheet; spread evenly with mayonnaise. Layer roast beef slices evenly over mayonnaise. Top with onion slices; cover with cheese. Bake at 450 degrees for 8 minutes, or until crust is golden and cheese is melted. Top with lettuce and tomato; cut into wedges and serve. Makes 4 servings.

After Sunday dinner, set up old-fashioned games like badminton and croquet in the backyard...fun for all ages! Indoors, try favorite board games. Everyone is sure to have a great time together.

Mom's Best
Sunday Suppers

Beef & Mushrooms on Biscuits
Sheila Wilson
Waco, TX

This recipe is absolutely delicious...great to enjoy for brunch or an evening meal. Quick & easy to prepare on a busy schedule. You can also replace the cream of mushroom soup with cream of chicken soup...use lean ground turkey or chicken instead of beef. I just used what I had on hand, and it was amazing. I am very proud of this recipe creation...it's featured on my blog, welcometomykitchen.net.

7-1/2 oz. tube refrigerated
  biscuits
1/2 green or red pepper, diced
1/2 onion, diced
1 t. oil or butter
1 lb. ground beef
10-3/4 oz. can cream of
  mushroom soup

4-oz. can sliced mushrooms,
  drained
1 t. garlic, minced
1 t. Italian seasoning
salt and pepper to taste

Bake biscuits according to package instructions. Meanwhile, in a skillet over medium heat, sauté pepper and onion in oil or butter until slightly softened. Add beef and cook until browned; drain. Add remaining ingredients; mix well. Simmer over medium-low heat for 10 minutes. To serve, split biscuits in half and place on 4 dinner plates; spoon beef mixture over biscuits. Makes 4 servings.

Food for friends doesn't have to be fancy. Invite everyone
to help themselves from large platters set right on
the table...so family-friendly!

Casual Sunday Suppers

Chilly-Night Skillet Lasagna
Terri Christiansen
Montague, MI

It gets cold here in Michigan, so I like to make this simple dish in the wintertime. I sometimes add black olives.

1 lb. ground beef
2-1/2 c. water
30-oz. jar spaghetti sauce
3 c. penne pasta, uncooked

1/2 t. Italian seasoning
4-1/2 oz. jar sliced mushrooms, drained

Brown beef in a large skillet over medium heat; drain. Stir in remaining ingredients. Bring to a boil, stirring occasionally. Reduce heat to low. Simmer, uncovered, for 10 to 12 minutes, until pasta is tender. Makes 6 servings.

Pork Sausage Meatballs
Amy Theisen
Sauk Rapids, MN

These meatballs are delicious served with a baked potato and a fresh vegetable. I like to add them to spaghetti sauce, too.

16-oz. pkg. ground Italian or regular pork sausage
1/3 c. dry bread crumbs or instant oats, uncooked

1/2 c. onion, finely chopped
1/4 c. grated Parmesan cheese
1 egg, lightly beaten
1/4 t. pepper

In a large bowl, mix all ingredients until blended. Shape into 12, 2-inch meatballs. Arrange meatballs in a single layer in a lightly greased 13"x9" shallow baking pan. Bake, uncovered, at 375 degrees for 15 minutes, or until cooked through. Serve as is, or add to favorite spaghetti sauce. Makes 4 servings.

Dip your hands into cold water before shaping meatballs...the meat won't stick to your hands.

Mom's Best
Sunday Suppers

Corny Hot Dog Casserole

Constance Bockstoce
Dallas, GA

An easy one-dish meal for hungry kids.
Economical and delicious!

8-1/2 oz. pkg. corn muffin mix
2 eggs, beaten
3/4 c. milk
1/2 c. onion, diced
1 T. dried celery flakes

1/2 t. pepper
15-oz. can corn, drained
1 lb. hot dogs, cut into bite-size
   pieces
1 c. shredded Cheddar cheese

In a large bowl, stir together dry muffin mix, eggs, milk, onion, celery flakes and pepper. Mix in corn, hot dogs and cheese. Spread mixture into a buttered 9"x9" baking pan or 2-quart casserole dish. Bake, uncovered, at 350 degrees for about 30 minutes, until batter sets. Serve warm. Makes 4 to 6 servings.

A fun and simple meal...try a chili dog bar! Along with steamed hot dogs and buns, set out chili, shredded cheese, sauerkraut, chopped onions and your favorite condiments.

Casual Sunday Suppers

Mom's Taco Casserole

Amanda Sandefur
Sarasota, FL

One of my mom's delicious recipes! We always enjoy
this dish served over crunchy tortilla chips.

1-1/2 lbs. ground beef, browned
  and drained
14-1/2 oz. can diced tomatoes
  with green chiles, drained
10-3/4 oz. can cream of onion
  soup
1-1/4 oz. pkg. taco seasoning
  mix

1/4 c. water
6 6-inch corn tortillas, cut into
  1/2-inch strips
1/2 c. sour cream
1 c. shredded Cheddar cheese
Garnish: 3 green onions, sliced

Combine beef, tomatoes, onion soup, seasoning mix and water in a
4-quart slow cooker. Gently stir in tortilla strips. Cover and cook on
low setting for 6 to 7 hours. Spread sour cream over top; sprinkle with
cheese. Cover and let stand for 5 minutes, or until cheese is melted.
Sprinkle with onions and serve. Serves 4.

A speedy side for any south-of-the-border supper. Stir spicy salsa
and shredded cheese into hot cooked rice. Cover and let stand a
few minutes, until the cheese melts. Sure to please!

Mom's Best
Sunday Suppers

One-Dish Fish Dinner

Cheri Maxwell
Gulf Breeze, FL

A light meal we enjoy on warm days, prepared in the microwave.
Serve with cooked rice or orzo pasta.

1 lb. cod, haddock or other white
    fish fillets, thawed if frozen
5 green onions, sliced
2 zucchini, sliced 1/4-inch thick
1/2 lb. sliced mushrooms
3 T. butter, melted

1 t. lemon juice
1/2 t. dried oregano
1/4 t. salt
1/8 t. pepper
2 ripe tomatoes, each cut into
    6 wedges

In a microwave-safe oval dish, arrange fish fillets with the thinnest parts to the center. Top with onions, zucchini and mushrooms; set aside. In a cup, combine melted butter, lemon juice and seasonings; drizzle over top. Cover tightly with plastic wrap. Microwave on high for 5 minutes. Rotate dish 1/2 turn, if not using a carousel. Microwave another 6 to 8 minutes, until fish flakes easily with a fork and vegetables are fork-tender. Add tomatoes to dish. Cover and microwave one to 2 minutes, until tomatoes are heated through. Serves 4.

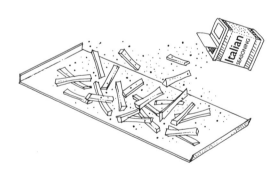

For zesty French fries that are anything but boring, spray frozen fries with non-stick olive oil spray and sprinkle with your favorite spice blend like Italian, Cajun or steak seasoning. spread on a baking sheet and bake as directed.

Casual Sunday Suppers

Simple Shrimp Scampi

Tamara Long
Huntsville, AR

My daughter has a beef allergy, so I've had to find fast, filling and yummy recipes to make for her whenever we were having burgers or steak. This is one of her favorites, even now that she is grown. If it's not saucy enough for you, increase the butter to 1/2 cup.

8-oz. pkg. angel hair pasta,
   uncooked
1/4 c. butter
1-1/2 t. to 1 T. garlic, chopped
Optional: 1/4 c. white wine

16-oz. pkg. frozen shrimp,
   peeled and cleaned
salt and pepper to taste
Optional: 1/8 t. red pepper flakes

Cook pasta according to package directions. Drain; allow to rest in colander. Add butter to pasta pot and allow to melt; stir in garlic and wine, if using. Rinse frozen shrimp, but do not thaw; add to mixture in pan. Cook over medium-low heat for about 5 minutes, until pink. Return pasta to pot and toss; season with salt, pepper and pepper flakes, if using. Makes 4 servings.

Cut flowers in a Mason jar are so cheerful on the dinner table. Group together jars of different heights for an appealing arrangement.

Mom's Best
Sunday Suppers

Cheesy Burger Bake

Diane Bertosa
Brunswick Hills, OH

This is one of the first recipes I made when I was married, many years ago. It's become one of our favorite comfort foods.

1 lb. ground beef
1/2 c. onion, chopped
2 T. mustard
1 t. salt
16 slices white bread, toasted
1/2 c. butter, softened
1 c. shredded mozzarella cheese

1 c. shredded Cheddar cheese
2 eggs, lightly beaten
1-1/2 c. milk
1 t. salt
1/8 to 1/4 t. pepper, to taste
1/4 t. dry mustard
paprika to taste

In a skillet over medium heat, cook beef with onion until browned. Drain; stir in mustard and salt. Meanwhile, toast bread slices; spread with butter. Combine cheeses in a bowl; set aside. In a greased 13"x9" baking pan, arrange 8 toast slices; top with half each of beef mixture and cheese mixture. Repeat layering; set aside. In a bowl, whisk together remaining ingredients except paprika. Spoon over layers in pan; sprinkle with paprika. Bake, uncovered, at 350 degrees for 30 to 35 minutes, until golden and cheese is melted. Serves 8.

When preparing a favorite casserole, it's easy to make a double batch. After baking, let the extra casserole cool, wrap well and tuck it in the freezer...ready to share with a new mother, carry to a potluck or reheat on a busy night at home.

Casual Sunday Suppers

Chicken & Spinach Quiche

Irene Robinson
Cincinnati, OH

Some evenings we enjoy having breakfast for dinner. This is
a great choice along with fresh fruit and warm dinner rolls.

9-inch deep-dish pie crust,
   unbaked
2 eggs, beaten
3/4 c. milk
3/4 c. mayonnaise
1/2 t. dried basil
1/2 t. salt

1/2 t. pepper
1 c. cooked chicken, chopped
1 c. shredded Swiss cheese
1/2 c. onion, chopped
2 T. grated Parmesan cheese
6-oz. pkg. baby spinach

Bake pie crust at 375 degrees for 10 minutes; cool slightly. Meanwhile,
in a bowl, whisk together eggs, milk, mayonnaise and seasonings. Fold
in remaining ingredients; pour into baked crust. Bake, uncovered, at
375 degrees for 40 minutes, or until set. Cool slightly; cut into wedges.
Makes 6 servings.

Make a quick crumb crust for a savory quiche. Spread
2-1/2 tablespoons softened butter in a pie plate, then firmly
press 2-1/2 cups seasoned dry bread crumbs into the butter.
Freeze until firm, pour in filling and bake as directed.

Mom's Best
Sunday Suppers

Chili Hominy Bake

Monty Rae Miles
Medford, OR

Perfect for a quick supper, as most of the ingredients can be kept on hand in the pantry. Serve with warm cornbread or sourdough bread.

1 lb. lean ground beef
1/2 c. onion, chopped
15-1/2 oz. can chili with beans
15-1/2 oz. can yellow hominy, drained
10-3/4 oz. can cream of chicken soup

2-1/4 oz. can sliced black olives, drained
1 T. chili powder
1/2 c. shredded Cheddar cheese

Brown beef with onion in a skillet over medium heat; drain. Add remaining ingredients except cheese. Mix well and transfer to a lightly greased 2-1/2 quart casserole dish. Bake, covered, at 350 degrees for 30 minutes. Top with cheese and bake, uncovered, for 5 minutes, until cheese melts. Makes 4 servings.

Potato Tot Casserole

Kathy Rivard
Southmayd, TX

My mom used to make this dish for us on school nights. It's very filling...real comfort food!

1 lb. ground beef
10-3/4 oz. can cream of chicken soup
10-3/4 oz. can cream of mushroom soup

14-1/2 oz. can cut green beans, drained
2 to 3 c. frozen potato puffs
2 to 3 slices American cheese, torn into pieces

Brown beef in a skillet over medium heat; drain. Transfer to a sprayed one-quart casserole dish. Mix soups and beans in a large bowl; spread over beef. Arrange enough potato puffs over soup mixture to cover. Top with cheese. Bake, uncovered, at 350 degrees for about 30 minutes, or until hot and bubbly and cheese is melted. Serves 8.

Casual Sunday Suppers

Quick Sunday Supper

Katie Majeske
Denver, PA

This is one of my favorite meals that Mom used to make. I fix it often for my own family because it's quick, easy and good.

1 lb. ground beef
1/2 c. onion, chopped
1/2 c. celery, chopped
10-3/4 oz. can cream of chicken
    or mushroom soup

10 T. water
1 t. Worcestershire sauce
5-oz. can chow mein noodles

In a skillet over medium heat, brown beef with onion and celery; drain. Stir in soup, water and Worcestershire sauce; simmer until heated through. Serve over chow mein noodles. Serves 6.

Keep a notepad on the fridge to make a note whenever a pantry staple is used up...you'll never run out of that one item you need for dinner.

Mom's Best
Sunday Suppers

Shantelle's Fabulous Chicken Fingers

Shirl Parsons
Cape Carteret, NC

This is my daughter's recipe...it's a family favorite!

4 chicken breasts, skin removed
   if desired
1/2 c. butter, melted
3/4 c. fine dry bread crumbs

1/4 c. grated Parmesan cheese
1/4 t. dried basil
1/4 t. dried thyme
3/4 t. salt

Cut each chicken breast in half, then into finger-length pieces. Add melted butter to a small bowl. In another bowl, mix remaining ingredients; mix well. Dip chicken pieces in butter, then into bread crumb mixture. Arrange on an ungreased aluminum foil-lined baking sheet. Bake at 400 degrees for 25 to 30 minutes, until golden and cooked through. Serves 6 to 8.

Sweet potato fries are delicious with casual meals. Slice sweet potatoes into wedges, toss with olive oil and place on a baking sheet. Bake at 400 degrees for 20 to 30 minutes until crisp and tender, turning once. Sprinkle with a little cinnamon-sugar and serve warm.

Simple Soup Suppers

Mom's Best
Sunday Suppers

Cowboy Stew

Jenna Harmon
Dolores, CO

After my husband and I married in 2009, my mother-in-law gave me the base to the recipe I have developed here. She made up this recipe when my husband was little, and then passed it on to me. Over the years, I've learned to customize it and make it my own way. I just recently shared my version of her recipe back to her, since she loves this version also!

2 lbs. stew beef cubes
2 T. plus 1 t. beef soup base
1 T. onion powder
1 T. garlic powder
1 t. salt
1 t. white pepper
3 cloves garlic, minced
3 lbs. redskin potatoes, cut
   into 3/4-inch cubes

3 c. cocktail vegetable juice,
   divided
1 sweet onion, chopped
1 green pepper, chopped
2 to 3 stalks celery, chopped
2 14-1/2 oz. cans cut green
   beans
2 15-1/4 oz. cans corn

In a 6 to 7-quart slow cooker, layer ingredients as follows: beef cubes, soup base, seasonings, garlic, potatoes, 1-1/2 cups vegetable juice, onion, green pepper, celery, green beans with liquid, corn with liquid and remaining vegetable juice. Add enough hot water to fill crock 3/4 full. Cover and cook on low setting for 9 to 10 hours. Makes 8 servings.

Make a family recipe book of all the best handed-down family favorites. Tie it all up with a bow and slip a family photo in the front...a gift to be treasured.

Simple Soup Suppers

Santa Fe Chicken Soup

Leona Krivda
Belle Vernon, PA

I love slow-cooker soups! They are so easy to make, great for a chilly-day fall or winter meal. This one is good with cornbread.

4 chicken breasts
garlic powder, onion powder,
   salt and pepper to taste
1/2 c. onion, finely chopped
14-1/2 oz. can diced tomatoes
10-oz. can diced tomatoes with
   green chiles

15-1/4 oz. can corn
2 15-oz. cans black beans,
   drained and lightly rinsed
16-oz. pkg. pasteurized process
   cheese, cubed
1/4 c. milk

In a large saucepan, cover chicken with water. Simmer over medium heat for 15 minutes, or until chicken is no longer pink in the center. Turn off heat; allow chicken to cool in broth. Shred chicken, discarding skin and bones; add seasonings as desired. In a 6-quart slow cooker, combine chicken, onion, undrained tomatoes, undrained corn, beans, cheese and milk; mix together well. Cover and cook on low setting for 3 to 4 hours, until bubbly and cheese is melted. If soup begins to boil, leave the lid off slightly until it returns to simmering. Makes 10 to 12 servings.

When serving soup or chili, offer guests a variety of fun toppings. Fill bowls with shredded cheese, oyster crackers, chopped onions, sour cream and crunchy croutons, then invite everyone to dig in!

Farmers' Market Vegetable Soup

Vickie
Gooseberry Patch

I just love to shop at our town's Saturday farmers' market. Often I get carried away, just looking at all the ripe produce, and try to bring it all home. When that happens, I make this tasty, easy soup. Feel free to mix & match your favorite veggies! For a vegetarian soup, use vegetable broth instead of chicken.

2 T. extra-virgin olive oil
3 carrots, peeled and diced
3 stalks celery, diced
1 onion, diced
1 leek, white part only, trimmed
   and thinly sliced
1 clove garlic, minced
1 potato, peeled and diced
4 roma tomatoes, diced

4 c. chicken broth
1/2 c. dry white wine or
   chicken broth
1 bay leaf
1 c. fresh or frozen green beans,
   chopped
1 T. fresh thyme, snipped
salt and pepper to taste

Heat olive oil in a stockpot over medium heat. Add carrots, celery, onion, leek and garlic; cook and stir for 2 to 3 minutes, until onion is translucent. Add potato and tomatoes; cook and stir for one more minute. Add chicken broth, wine or broth and bay leaf; increase heat to medium-high and bring to a boil. Reduce heat to medium-low; simmer for 15 minutes, stirring occasionally. Add green beans and thyme. Cook for another 10 minutes, or until potato and beans are tender. Discard bay leaf; season with salt and pepper. Makes 4 to 6 servings.

It's best to remove bay leaves before serving your soup or stew. Tuck them into a metal tea ball that can hang on the side of the soup pot...easy to remove when done.

Simple Soup Suppers

Mom's Best Chili

Lori Dom
Martinsburg, WV

My mom was famous for taking what she has on hand and making a delicious dish. Her chili recipe is a great way to get added vegetables...it's one of my favorite meals.

1 lb. ground beef
1 c. onion, diced
1/2 c. celery, diced
1/2 c. carrot, peeled and
   finely diced
4 c. tomato juice

15-oz. can tomato sauce
14-1/2 oz. can diced tomatoes
   with green chiles
2 T. sugar
15-1/2 oz. can kidney beans
2 T. chili powder, or to taste

In a large soup pot over medium heat, cook beef with onion, celery and carrot until beef is browned and vegetables are softened. Drain; stir in tomato juice, tomato sauce, tomatoes with juice and sugar. Bring to a boil; reduce heat to medium-low and simmer for 20 to 30 minutes. Stir in kidney beans and chili powder; simmer for 10 minutes, or until heated through. Makes 6 servings.

Top bowls of soup with crunchy cheese toasts. Brush thin slices of French bread with olive oil. Broil for 2 to 3 minutes, until golden. Turn over and sprinkle with freshly grated Parmesan cheese and Italian seasoning. Broil another 2 to 3 minutes, until cheese melts. Yum!

Mom's Best
Sunday Suppers

Mom's Slow-Cooker Ham & Bean Soup

Diane Brulc
Brookfield, WI

My mom always made her famous soup. We enjoyed it served over hot cooked rice, topped with our favorite catsup. I have made it this way for more than 50 years.

1-1/2 c. dried Great Northern
    beans, rinsed and sorted
8 c. water
1 meaty ham bone
2 potatoes, peeled and cut into
    1-1/2 inch cubes
2 to 3 carrots, peeled and
    finely chopped
2 stalks celery with leaves,
    finely chopped
1 c. onion, chopped

8 c. water
1 T . dried parsley
2 t. garlic powder
1/4 t. ground cloves
1 bay leaf
1 t. salt
1/2 t. pepper
2 c. cooked ham, cut into
    1/2-inch cubes
cooked rice
Garnish: catsup

Cover beans with water; soak overnight. Drain and rinse; transfer beans to a slow cooker. Add 8 cups fresh water, ham bone, vegetables and seasonings. Cover and cook on low setting for 8 hours. Discard ham bone and bay leaf; stir in cubed ham. Continue to cook for another 30 minutes to one hour. Serve in bowls over hot cooked rice, topped with catsup. Makes 6 servings.

Mom's secret to the most delicious home-cooked soup?
Taste as you go, adding more salt, pepper and other
seasonings as the soup simmers.

Simple Soup Suppers

Easy Chicken & Rice Soup with Tomatoes

Teresa Mosley
Lorena, TX

A very special friend shared this recipe with me and every time I make it, I think of her. My husband loves it and takes it to work for lunch regularly. This soup is actually better on the second and third days, after the flavors have blended together.

2 19-oz. cans chicken & rice
  soup with vegetables
14-1/2 oz. can diced tomatoes
  with green chiles
15-1/2 oz. can Great Northern
  beans, drained and rinsed

2-1/2 lb. deli rotisserie chicken,
  bones and skin removed
1/8 t. garlic powder
1/8 t. onion powder
Optional: chicken broth or water,
  as needed

In a large Dutch oven over medium heat, combine chicken & rice soup, tomatoes with juice and beans. Add chicken and seasonings; stir well. Bring to a boil; reduce heat to medium-low and simmer for about 20 to 30 minutes. If more liquid is needed, add a little chicken broth or water. Makes 6 to 8 servings.

Beefy Vegetable Soup

Gloria Kaufmann
Orrville, OH

It's easy to keep the ingredients for this tasty soup in the freezer and pantry for a last-minute meal.

1-1/2 lbs. ground beef chuck
1/2 c. onion, chopped
salt and pepper to taste
2 12-oz. pkgs. frozen
  mixed vegetables

46-oz. can tomato juice
2 to 3 cubes beef bouillon
Optional: beef broth or water,
  as needed

Brown beef with onion in a skillet over medium heat. Drain; season with salt and pepper. Meanwhile, in a soup pot, cook vegetables according to package directions; drain. Add beef mixture, tomato juice and bouillon to vegetables; simmer until heated through. Thin soup with a little beef broth or water, if desired. Serves 8.

Mom's Best
Sunday Suppers

5-Bean Chicken Stew

Lisanne Miller
Wells, ME

This recipe feeds a crowd on a cold day. This stew is requested more often than anything else I make...if only they knew how easy it is! Add some chopped jalapeños, if you like it hot.

2 to 3 boneless, skinless chicken breasts
3 14-1/2 oz. cans crushed tomatoes
11-oz. can sweet corn & diced peppers, drained
15-1/2 oz. can ranch-style beans
15-1/2 oz. can black beans
15-1/2 oz. can kidney beans
15-1/2 oz. can chili beans
15-1/2 oz. can red beans
1/2 c. onion, finely chopped
1 t. garlic, minced
11-oz. pkg. tortilla chips, crushed
Garnish: shredded Cheddar cheese, sour cream

Place chicken in a 6-quart slow cooker. Add tomatoes with juice, corn, all cans of beans, onion and garlic. Cover and cook on low setting for 7 to 8 hours, until chicken is tender and shreds easily. Shred chicken in crock with 2 forks; stir into mixture in crock. To serve, ladle soup into bowls over a bed of crushed tortilla chips; top with shredded cheese and sour cream. Makes 8 servings.

There's nothing cozier than a bowl of warm soup. For extra comfort, warm up oven-safe bowls in a 200-degree oven before filling...the soup (and guests) will stay warmer longer!

Simple Soup Suppers

Speedy Taco Soup

Linda Peterson
Mason, OH

One of my favorite soup recipes...simple to make in an electric pressure cooker! Serve topped with sour cream, sliced avocado and a side of tortilla chips. Yum!

1 lb. ground beef or
    ground turkey
2 T. olive oil
1 c. onion, diced
2 T. taco seasoning mix
1 T. ranch salad dressing mix
14-1/2 oz. can stewed tomatoes
14-1/2 oz. can petite diced
    tomatoes

15-1/2 oz. can kidney beans,
    drained
15-1/2 oz. can pinto beans,
    drained
8-oz. can tomato sauce
1 c. canned or frozen corn
4-oz. can diced green chiles
2-1/4 oz. can sliced black olives,
    drained

Set electric pressure cooker on Sauté and start to brown beef with olive oil. Stir in onion and seasoning mixes. Continue to brown beef until no pink remains and onion is slightly softened. Stir in tomatoes with juice and remaining ingredients. Secure lid and set to Sealing. Select Manual/Pressure and cook for 6 minutes at high pressure. After cooking time is up, let pressure release naturally for 5 minutes. Use Venting/Quick Release method to release remaining pressure. Open carefully; stir again and serve. Makes 6 servings.

Keep the cupboard tidy...tuck packets of salad and seasoning mix into a vintage napkin holder.

Mom's Best
Sunday Suppers

Jo's Escarole, Bean & Sausage Soup

JoAnne Wilson
Roselle Park, NJ

This soup is quick, easy and satisfying. Great for supper year 'round... my husband, son and whole family love it! It's good as a cool-weather comfort meal or a light and easy stovetop summer dinner. Serve with a fresh garden salad and warm crusty bread.

1/2 c. sweet onion, diced
1 stalk celery, diced
1 to 2 carrots, peeled and diced
1 T. oil
1 lb. ground Italian pork sausage with fennel
Optional: fennel seeds to taste
4 c. water
1-1/2 T. lower-sodium roasted chicken soup base
14-1/2 oz. can diced tomatoes

2 15-1/2 oz. cans Great Northern beans, drained and rinsed
1 to 2 T. fresh parsley, chopped
1 to 2 T. fresh basil, thinly sliced
1 to 2 bunches fresh escarole, chopped
8-oz. pkg. long fusilli pasta, uncooked and broken
2 to 3 t. butter
Garnish: shredded Pecorino Romano cheese

In a large soup pot over medium heat, sauté onion, celery and carrots in oil until soft. Add sausage and cook until no longer pink, breaking up while cooking; add fennel seeds, if desired. Stir in water, soup base, tomatoes with juice, beans, parsley and basil. Simmer over medium-low heat for about 20 minutes. Stir in escarole and simmer 10 minutes longer. Meanwhile, cook pasta according to package directions; drain and toss with butter. (Keep pasta separate from soup until serving time, or it will get mushy and soak up all the broth.) To serve, place cooked pasta in soup bowls and ladle soup over top. Top with shredded Pecorino Romano cheese. Serves 4.

Need to add a little zing to a pot of soup? Just add a splash of vinegar or lemon juice.

Simple Soup Suppers

Nanita's Pork Green Chile Stew

Alicia Salazar-Samuels
Parker, CO

My mom's green chile stew is like a great big hug on a cold winter's evening. You can make this wonderful stew as mild or as hot as you like, depending on your taste. Either way, the flavor is amazing and always a hit at my house. Serve with a side of warm tortillas. Make sure to save some to spoon over scrambled eggs in the morning!

2 lbs. boneless pork, cubed
salt and pepper to taste
2 T. oil
3/4 c. white onion, diced
2 to 3 cloves garlic, chopped
1/4 c. all-purpose flour
14-1/2 oz. can diced tomatoes
   with green chiles

32-oz. container low-sodium
   chicken broth
1 T. tomato-chicken bouillon
   granules
1 lb. flame-roasted whole Hatch
   or Pueblo green chiles,
   peeled, seeded and chopped

Season pork with salt and pepper. In a large oven-safe Dutch oven over medium heat, brown pork in oil. Add onion and garlic; cook and stir until fragrant, 2 to 3 minutes. Sprinkle with flour and cook an additional 2 minutes, being careful not to scorch flour. Add tomatoes with juice, chicken broth and bouillon. Cover and bake at 325 degrees for about 2 hours, until pork is tender. Remove from oven; add chiles and simmer on stovetop for 30 minutes. Taste and adjust seasonings, as necessary. Makes 6 to 7 servings.

To roast green chiles: place whole chiles on a broiler pan. Broil until blackened on all sides, turning with tongs. Transfer chiles to a bowl and cover tightly with plastic wrap. Let stand for about 15 minutes; skin should peel off easily. Discard skin and seeds; cut chiles into strips.

Pick up a dozen pint Mason jars...
they're perfect for serving cold
beverages at informal gatherings.

Mom's Best
Sunday Suppers

Cabbage & Beef Soup

Marie Stowers
Raleigh, NC

This recipe came from my late sister-in-law Shirlene, who was a wonderful cook and shared with our large family many of her wonderful creations. It's an easy dish for stovetop or slow cooker...so good on a cold day! This soup can be frozen in serving-size portions for later enjoyment.

1/2 to 1 lb. lean ground beef
3/4 c. onion, chopped
1/4 c. green pepper, chopped
14-1/2 oz. can chili-ready
    tomatoes
14-1/2 oz. can diced tomatoes
14-1/2 oz. can chili beans

1/2 head cabbage, chopped
1 stalk celery, chopped
3-1/2 c. water
4 cubes beef bouillon
1/4 t. garlic powder
1/2 t. garlic salt
1/4 t. pepper

In a soup pot over medium heat, brown beef with onion and green pepper; drain. Add undrained tomatoes and beans; stir in remaining ingredients. Bring to a boil. Reduce heat to medium-low; cover and simmer for one hour, stirring occasionally. May also be prepared in a slow cooker; combine beef mixture and remaining ingredients in slow cooker. Cover and cook on low setting for 4 hours, or until cabbage is tender. Makes 8 servings.

Leftover soup after supper? Ladle 2-cup portions into freezer bags...seal, label and freeze. Then, whenever you need a quick-fix meal another day, simply let family members choose a bag, transfer soup to a microwave-safe bowl and reheat.

Simple Soup Suppers

Chili Con Carne

Michele Shenk
Manheim, PA

My sister-in-law Kathy gave me this recipe years ago, after my children came home from her house saying how delicious it was! It's one of our favorites. We enjoy it plain or served over rice.

1 lb. ground beef
1 onion, minced
2 cloves garlic, minced
1 T. all-purpose flour
2 t. chili powder
1-1/2 t. salt
1 to 2 14-1/2 oz. cans
    diced tomatoes

1/2 c. hot water
15-1/2 oz. can kidney beans,
    drained
Garnish: sour cream, shredded
    Cheddar cheese

In a large skillet over medium heat, brown beef with onion and garlic; drain. Mix flour, chili powder and salt; stir into beef mixture. Add tomatoes with juice and water. Cover and simmer over medium-low heat for one hour, stirring occasionally. Add a little more water, if necessary. Add beans and bring to a boil. Serve topped with sour cream and shredded cheese. Makes 6 to 8 servings.

A fast & fun new way to serve cornbread! Mix up the batter, thin slightly with a little extra liquid, then bake until crisp in a waffle iron. Cut into strips...terrific for dunking in chili.

Mom's Best
Sunday Suppers

Creamy Wild Rice Soup

Joanne Mauseth
Clear Lake, SD

This soup is a great way to enjoy the last little bit of the baked ham from a previous meal. For a different flavor, roast chicken can also be used...delicious either way! Garnish with a dollop of sour cream.

1-1/2 c. water
1/2 t. salt
1/2 c. wild rice, uncooked
6 T. butter
3 T. green onions, diced
1/3 c. all-purpose flour

4 c. chicken broth
1/2 c. cooked ham, chopped
1/4 c. carrots, peeled and
   finely grated
1/4 t. pepper
1 c. half-and-half

In a large saucepan over medium heat, bring water and salt to a boil. Add rice and return to a boil. Reduce heat to medium-low; cover and simmer for 50 to 55 minutes. Let stand for 10 minutes; drain. Melt butter in a medium saucepan over medium heat; sauté onions. Blend in flour; gradually stir in chicken broth. Cook, stirring constantly, until mixture comes to a boil. Continue to boil for one minute. Stir in cooked rice, ham, carrots and pepper; simmer for 5 minutes. Just before serving, blend in half-and-half; heat through, but do not boil. Makes 4 servings.

The earthy, nutty flavor of wild rice is delicious in soups, salads and sides. When shopping, be sure not to mistake it for already-seasoned mixes of wild rice and long-grain rice.

Simple Soup Suppers

Broccoli-Cheese Soup

Janet Rettig
Ward, AR

This is the best broccoli soup you will ever taste...it is so good on a cold winter day! My mom has made this soup for years, and now I use her recipe too.

1/2 c. butter
16-oz. pkg. frozen chopped
  broccoli, thawed
2 to 3 potatoes, peeled
  and chopped
3 stalks celery, chopped
3 carrots, peeled and chopped

1 onion, chopped
3 14-oz. cans chicken broth
2 10-3/4 oz. cans cream of
  chicken soup
16-oz. pkg. pasteurized process
  cheese spread, cubed
8-oz. container sour cream

Melt butter in a large soup pot over medium heat; add broccoli, potatoes, celery, carrots and onion. Sauté until tender, stirring occasionally. Add chicken broth and simmer over low heat for 30 minutes, stirring often. Stir in chicken soup and simmer for 10 minutes, stirring often. Add cheese and simmer, stirring constantly, until cheese is melted. Remove from heat. Just before serving, stir in sour cream. Makes 10 servings.

Don't hesitate to use frozen vegetables in homemade soup. Flash-frozen quickly after being harvested, they often retain more nutrients than fresh produce. And, they're available in many varieties, trimmed and chopped, all ready to add to a pot of soup.

Mom's Best
Sunday Suppers

Chicken Vegetable Soup

Barbara Treat
Ennis, TX

This is a family favorite from my grandmother, whom we all called Mom. I like to add some sliced black olives and serve it with a salad and garlic toast. It's easy, quick and delicious!

12-oz. can chicken, flaked
15-oz. can mixed vegetables,
    drained and rinsed
16-oz. can whole potatoes,
    drained, rinsed and diced
3-1/4 c. water
1-1/2 t. garlic salt, or to taste

0.6-oz. pkg. cream of chicken
    soup mix
8-oz. pkg. pasteurized process
    cheese spread, diced
10-3/4 oz. can Cheddar cheese
    soup, divided

In a soup pot, combine undrained chicken and remaining ingredients, adding just half of cheese soup. (Reserve remaining soup for another use.) Stir well and cook over medium heat until heated through. Makes 6 servings.

Mark's Chili

Mark Rushlow
Westland, MI

My kids always liked this chili because it's not overly spicy. Sometimes for an extra twist, I add a little brown sugar and cola. Yummy!

1-1/2 lbs. ground beef chuck
3/4 c. white onion, chopped
1 green pepper, chopped
14-1/2 oz. can tomato sauce
1-1/4 oz. pkg. mild chili
    seasoning mix

2 14-1/2 oz. cans diced tomatoes
16-oz. can refried beans
15-1/2 oz. can mild chili beans
15-1/2 oz. can black beans
15-1/2 oz. can pinto beans

In a skillet over medium heat, brown beef with onion and green pepper; drain. Stir in tomato sauce and seasoning mix; transfer to a 6-quart slow cooker. Add undrained tomatoes and beans; stir. Cover and cook on low setting for 4 hours. Makes 8 to 10 servings.

Simple Soup Suppers

Baked Chicken Chili

Candace Eshkakogan
Ontario, Canada

Baking this chili in the oven makes the difference! Add as much spice as you want, and whatever spice you prefer. Serve with warm bread or crackers.

1 lb. ground chicken
3/4 c. onion, chopped
2 stalks celery, chopped
Optional: 2 to 3 t. oil
28-oz. can diced tomatoes
16-oz. can baked beans in
    tomato sauce

16-oz. can red kidney beans
1/2 t. salt
1/2 t. pepper
garlic & herb seasoning to taste
chili powder to taste

Set a roasting pan on the stovetop over medium heat. Add chicken, onion, celery and oil, if needed; cook until chicken is browned and vegetables are tender. Add undrained tomatoes and beans; stir well. Mix in seasonings. Cover and bake at 275 degrees for 3 hours, stirring occasionally. Makes 5 servings.

Making grilled sandwiches to go with soup for supper? Get out Mom's cast-iron skillet for the tastiest, toastiest hot sandwiches. Cast iron provides even heat distribution for crisp golden crusts and speedy cooking.

Mom's Best
Sunday Suppers

Slow-Cooker Mushroom & Beef Barley Soup

Katie Bonomo
Ogden, IL

This soup is so delicious! Everyone who tastes it always asks for the recipe. Add some crusty bread to make it a hearty meal for a cold winter day.

1 to 2 T. oil
2 lbs. stew beef, cut into
   1-1/2 inch cubes
garlic powder, salt and pepper
   to taste
6 c. beef broth
6 stalks celery, chopped

3 carrots, peeled and chopped
2 4-oz. cans sliced mushrooms,
   drained
10-1/2 oz. can beef gravy
1 c. quick-cooking barley,
   uncooked

Heat oil in a large skillet over medium heat. Add beef cubes; season with garlic powder, salt and pepper. Cook beef on all sides, just until browned but not cooked through. Transfer beef to a 6-quart slow cooker. Stir in remaining ingredients except barley. Cover and cook on high setting for 5 to 6 hours, or on low setting for 8 to 9 hours. During the last 30 minutes of cooking, add barley and stir to combine; cover and cook until barley is tender. Makes 8 servings.

A flexible plastic cutting mat makes speedy work of slicing and dicing. Keep 2 mats on hand for chopping veggies and meat separately.

Simple Soup Suppers

Quick Italian Chicken & Bean Soup

Melissa Flasck
Rochester Hills, MI

This is a pressure-cooker recipe, but could also be simmered on the stovetop. Our deli grocery store sells rotisserie chicken already cut up and shredded. It's a great shortcut after a long day of work!

4 c. chicken broth
14-1/2 oz. can petite diced
  tomatoes
2 15-1/2 oz. cans cannellini
  beans, drained
1 T. garlic, minced
1 T. Italian seasoning

1 t. chili powder
1 t. salt
1 lb. deli rotisserie chicken,
  diced or shredded
Garnish: shredded Italian-blend
  cheese, sour cream

In an electric pressure cooker, combine all ingredients except chicken and garnish. Secure the lid and set the pressure release to Sealing. Use Manual/Pressure setting and cook for 5 minutes. When cooking time is up, use Venting/Quick Release. Open carefully; stir in chicken. Ladle soup into bowls; top with cheese and a dollop of sour cream. Makes 6 servings.

When you finish a chunk of aged Parmesan cheese, don't toss out the rind! Save it to add to a pot of soup for rich flavor.

Mom's Best
Sunday Suppers

Midwest Ham Chowder

Amy Daniels
Kalamazoo, MI

This was one of our favorite meals made by our amazing mom. My brother, sister and I now make it for our own families, who love it just as much. Serve with a crisp salad and warm, crusty bread...so good!

2 c. water
2 c. potatoes, peeled and cubed
1/2 c. carrots, peeled and sliced
1/2 c. celery, sliced
1/2 c. onion, diced
salt and pepper to taste
1/4 c. butter

1/4 c. all-purpose flour
2 c. milk
2-1/2 c. shredded sharp Cheddar
  cheese
14-3/4 oz. can cream-style corn
2 c. cooked ham, diced

In a large saucepan over medium heat, bring water to a boil. Add vegetables; season with salt and pepper. Cover and simmer 10 minutes, or until tender; do not drain. In another saucepan, melt butter over medium heat; whisk in flour. Add milk; cook and stir until thickened. Add cheese and stir until melted. Add cheese sauce, corn and ham to vegetable mixture. Mix well and heat through, but do not boil. Makes 6 servings.

Salt pork adds old-fashioned flavor to pots of soup, potatoes, green beans and navy beans. Look for it at the meat counter... if you don't find any, bacon or ham can be substituted.

Simple Soup Suppers

Pasta Fagioli with Cream

Mariann Raftery
New Rochelle, NY

A hearty soup with a dash of cream...tastes like a dream. I like this as a meatless soup, but for a heartier flavor, add a ham bone or some cooked sausage or bacon to the soup as it simmers.

16-oz. pkg. ditalini pasta, uncooked
2-1/2 T. olive oil
1 onion, chopped
1 stalk celery, chopped
4 cloves garlic, chopped
14-1/2 oz. can petite diced tomatoes
6 c. chicken broth

15-1/2 oz. can red or white kidney beans, drained and rinsed
1 T. fresh or dried basil, snipped
1 T. fresh or dried oregano, snipped
salt and pepper to taste
1/4 c. whipping cream
Garnish: grated Parmesan cheese

Cook pasta according to package directions; drain and set aside. (Do not add cooked pasta to the soup pot, or all the liquid will be absorbed.) Meanwhile, add olive oil to a separate large pot over medium heat. Sauté onion, celery and garlic until tender. Add tomatoes with juice; cook for 15 to 20 minutes. Stir in chicken broth, beans and seasonings. Reduce heat to medium-low; simmer for 30 minutes. Stir in cream. If more cream is desired, add 2 tablespoons at a time; stir well. To serve, ladle soup and pasta into soup bowls; top with grated cheese. Makes 6 to 8 servings.

Parsley, sage, rosemary, thyme...to enjoy the best flavor from your favorite fresh herbs, add them to recipes toward the end of the cooking period.

Mom's Best
Sunday Suppers

Quick & Easy Clam Chowder
Regina Vining
Warwick, RI

Quick to fix for a chilly Sunday evening supper! Serve with oyster crackers, or with my kids' favorite, cheesy goldfish crackers.

3 slices bacon
1 c. onion, chopped
2 c. chicken broth
4 c. potatoes, peeled and diced
3/4 c. celery, chopped
15-oz. can corn, drained
4 c. milk

6 T. all-purpose flour
1/2 t. salt
2 6-1/2 oz. cans chopped clams, drained
1/4 t. seafood seasoning or paprika

In a large saucepan over medium heat, cook bacon until crisp. Crumble bacon and set aside, reserving 2 teaspoons drippings in saucepan. Add onion and sauté until tender. Stir in chicken broth, potatoes, celery and corn. Cover and simmer for 15 minutes, or until vegetables are tender. In a bowl, whisk together milk, flour and salt to blend; add to broth mixture. Cook and stir over medium heat for 3 minutes, or until heated through and slightly thickened. Add clams and heat through. Top bowls of chowder with crumbled bacon and a sprinkle of seasoning. Serves 4.

Vintage tea towels are perfect for lining bread baskets.
They'll keep freshly baked rolls toasty warm and add
a dash of color to the table.

Simple Soup Suppers

Salmon Stew

Kerrie Crawford
Bessemer, AL

My momma, sister, brother and I couldn't wait until it got cold outside...we knew that it was time for delicious Salmon Stew. You can add ingredients like onion, carrots or cooked rice, but for us, plain is best! Enjoy it like we did, served with saltine crackers and slices of Cheddar cheese.

14-3/4 oz. can salmon, flaked
6 T. butter
3 12-oz. cans evaporated milk

Optional: grated onion and carrot
to taste

Remove skin and bones from salmon, as desired. Combine salmon and butter in a saucepan; heat until butter is melted. Add evaporated milk and optional ingredients, if desired; stir well. Bring to a boil over medium heat; reduce heat to medium-low and simmer for 5 minutes. Serves 4.

Tomato-Basil Bisque

Lori Rosenberg
Cleveland, OH

I grew up on canned tomato soup, but this is a quick, easy and healthy alternative. Tasty with grilled cheese sandwiches!

6 c. ripe tomatoes, coarsely
   chopped and seeds removed
15-oz. can tomato sauce

2 c. vegetable or chicken broth
1/4 c. fresh basil, snipped,
   or 2 t. dried basil

Working in batches, combine tomatoes, tomato sauce and broth in a blender. Process until smooth. Transfer to a saucepan; stir in basil. Heat through over medium heat and serve. Makes 4 to 6 servings.

Tickle little ones' taste buds with bowls of hot soup topped with cheesy popcorn.

Mom's Best
Sunday Suppers

Mom's Slovenian Stew

Mary Jean Willsey
Martinsville, IN

This is my mother's recipe for a hearty stew that originated in Slovenia. My grandparents immigrated from there in the 1800s. It is very tasty and satisfying, served with thick buttered slices of bread to sop up any sauce that's left in the bottom of the bowls.

2 T. oil
1 lb. stew beef cubes
1/4 c. all-purpose flour
1 c. celery, chopped
1 c. green pepper, chopped
1 banana pepper, chopped
2 cloves garlic, chopped
2 T. paprika
1 t. garlic powder

1-1/2 t. salt
1/4 t. pepper
28-oz. can diced tomatoes
12-oz. can tomato paste
3 carrots, peeled and chopped
3 potatoes, peeled and cubed
4 c. water, or 2 c. water plus
    12-oz. can beer
1 c. peas or green beans

Heat oil in a large Dutch oven over medium heat. Coat beef in flour and add to pan; brown on all sides. Add celery, peppers and garlic; sauté over low heat. Sprinkle with seasonings. Add tomatoes with juice and remaining ingredients except peas or beans; stir well. Simmer for 2 to 3 hours, stirring occasionally and adding more water, if necessary. Add peas or beans; cook another 15 minutes. Serves 4 to 5.

Mom often had a pot of savory soup bubbling on a back burner of the stove...use a slow cooker to cook up the same slow-simmered flavor! A favorite soup recipe that simmers for one to 2 hours on the stove can cook for 6 to 8 hours on the low setting without overcooking.

Simple Soup Suppers

Easy Chicken Stew

Patricia Nau
River Grove, IL

*This is such an easy and delicious recipe. My family loves it...
yours will, too! Serve with mashed potatoes, rice or noodles.*

10 chicken legs or thighs
paprika, salt and pepper to taste
3 T. shortening
2 10-oz. pkgs. frozen chopped
   onions

3 green peppers, diced
1 t. garlic, chopped
1-1/2 c. chicken broth
1 T. cornstarch
2 T. cold water or chicken broth

Season chicken pieces on all sides with paprika, salt and pepper. Place chicken in a large stockpot with a lid; set aside. Melt shortening in a non-stick skillet over medium heat; sauté onions and green peppers until onions are translucent. Add garlic and sauté for about 30 seconds. Add onion mixture and chicken broth to chicken in pan. Cover and simmer over low heat for 30 minutes, or until chicken is tender. Remove chicken pieces to a plate, reserving mixture in pan. Allow chicken to cool; chop or shred chicken, discarding skin and bones. Combine cornstarch and cold water in a cup; add to mixture in pan. Cook and stir until thickened. Season with additional salt and pepper, if desired. Return chicken to pot and simmer another 10 minutes. Makes 4 to 5 servings.

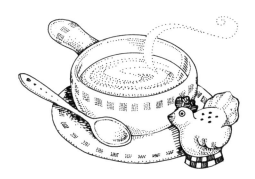

Bone-in, skin-on chicken makes the most flavorful chicken soup. Skin and bones are easily removed after the chicken is cooked. If you prefer, chill the soup overnight and skim off the fat before rewarming and serving.

Mom's Best
Sunday Suppers

Chicken & Patch Dumplings
Mary Donaldson
Enterprise, AL

My grandmother was the owner of a boardinghouse before I was born.
This is a dish she served her boarders and one of her favorites.

3 lbs. chicken breasts, or
    assorted chicken pieces
1 carrot, trimmed and peeled
1 small onion, peeled

1 stalk celery with leaves,
    trimmed
2 t. salt
1/2 t. pepper

In a large stockpot, combine all ingredients; add enough warm water to cover. Bring to a boil over medium-high heat; reduce heat to medium-low. Cover and simmer for 2 hours, or until chicken is tender. Remove chicken and vegetables from broth to a large bowl; set aside. Bring broth in pan to a low simmer. Chop chicken into bite-size pieces and add to broth. Drop Patch Dumplings into simmering broth. Cover and steam for 15 to 20 minutes; don't peek. Test dumplings for doneness and serve. Makes 4 to 5 servings.

Patch Dumplings:

1 c. all-purpose flour
1/2 t. salt
1/2 c. milk
2 T. canola oil or chicken fat

Optional: 1 T. celery leaves,
    finely chopped, or
    1/2 t. celery seed

Mix all ingredients until a soft dough forms. Roll out on a floured surface; cut into bit-size squares.

As an old French proverb says, to make good soup, the pot must only simmer, or "smile." As soon as the broth comes to a boil, turn down the heat to low. The soup will barely simmer, with bubbles breaking very gently on the surface.

Simple Soup Suppers

Easy Chicken-Broccoli Rice Soup

Courtney Stultz
Weir, KS

This rich and flavorful soup cooks up quickly in an electric pressure cooker. I love being able to sneak in lots of veggies with this soup! It's also easy to make in the slow cooker or on the stovetop.

2 boneless, skinless chicken
   breasts
3 c. chicken broth
1 c. wild rice, uncooked
1 c. milk
8-oz. pkg. sliced mushrooms
2 c. broccoli, chopped
1 c. carrots, peeled and diced

1 c. celery, diced
1 c. onion, diced
1 clove garlic, minced
2 t. dried thyme
2 t. dried parsley
1 t. dried oregano
1 t. salt
1/2 t. pepper

Add chicken breasts and chicken broth to an electric pressure cooker. Secure the lid; set pressure release to Sealing and cook on Manual/Pressure for 15 minutes. Use Venting/Quick Release method to release remaining pressure; open carefully and remove chicken. Shred chicken and return to pot; stir in remaining ingredients. Secure lid again; press the Soup setting and cook for 20 minutes. Quick-release pressure and let cool slightly before serving. Makes 6 servings.

Families are like branches on a tree. We may grow
in different directions, yet our roots remain as one.
– Unknown

Mom's Best
Sunday Suppers

Mom's Friendship Stew

Carolyn Deckard
Bedford, IN

This is our family's favorite stew. After my dad passed away, Mom would make this stew to share whenever she needed help with something around the house. It was always delicious with her homemade bread.

2 lbs. ground beef
4 14-1/2 oz. cans crushed
   Italian-style tomatoes
4 potatoes, peeled and coarsely
   chopped
1 onion, coarsely chopped
15-1/4 oz. can corn, drained
14-1/2 oz. can cut green beans,
   drained

14-1/2 oz. can sliced carrots,
   drained
1 t. dried oregano
2 t. salt
1 t. pepper
1 c. frozen peas

Brown beef in a large stockpot over medium heat; drain. Add tomatoes with juice and remaining ingredients except peas. Bring to a boil; reduce heat to medium-low. Simmer for 40 minutes, or until potatoes are tender, stirring occasionally. Add peas and cook 5 minutes longer. Serves 8.

A crock of homemade soup and a cheery bouquet
of flowers are sure pick-me-ups for a friend
who is feeling under the weather.

Simple Soup Suppers

Pat's Quick & Easy Loaded Potato Soup

Pat Beach
Fisherville, KY

After making this recipe the hard way for years by baking the potatoes and frying the bacon, I decided to make some changes. Substituting a bag of frozen hashbrowns for the potatoes and a package of real bacon bits for the fried bacon made this recipe so much easier to make, and it didn't change the flavor at all. This is definitely restaurant-quality potato soup. Enjoy!

2/3 c. margarine
2/3 c. all-purpose flour
7 c. milk
32-oz. pkg. frozen southern-
   style diced potatoes, thawed
4 green onions, chopped

3-oz. pkg. real bacon pieces
1-1/4 c. shredded Cheddar
   cheese
8-oz. container sour cream
1 t. salt
1 t. pepper

In a stockpot or Dutch oven, melt margarine over medium heat. Whisk in flour until smooth. Gradually stir in milk, whisking constantly, until thickened. Stir in potatoes and onions. Bring to a boil, stirring often. Reduce heat to medium-low; simmer for 8 to 10 minutes. Stir in remaining ingredients. Continue cooking, stirring constantly, until cheese is melted. Makes 6 servings.

Just for fun, serve up soft pretzels with soup instead of dinner rolls...so easy, the kids can do it! Twist strips of refrigerated bread stick dough into pretzel shapes and place on an ungreased baking sheet. Brush with beaten egg white, sprinkle with coarse salt and bake as the package directs.

Mom's Best
Sunday Suppers

Quick Split Pea & Ham Soup

Shirley Howie
Foxboro, MA

This is so easy to make...just drop everything into a pressure cooker! The result is a hearty, flavorful comfort soup. It will thicken as it cools, so you could add an extra cup of broth or water, if you wish.

1 lb. dried split peas, rinsed
   and sorted
1 c. celery, coarsely chopped
3 carrots, peeled and coarsely
   chopped
1 onion, coarsely chopped
2 cloves garlic, minced
1/2 lb. cooked ham steak, cubed

1 t. paprika
1 t. dried thyme
1/4 t. dried oregano
1/4 t. salt
1/2 t. pepper
2 bay leaves
6 c. chicken or vegetable broth

Add all ingredients to an electric pressure cooker; stir well to combine. Secure the lid and set the pressure release to Sealing. Use Manual/Pressure setting for 15 minutes. Allow a 10-minute natural pressure release. Turn the steam release handle to the venting position to release remaining pressure. Discard bay leaves and serve. Makes 6 servings.

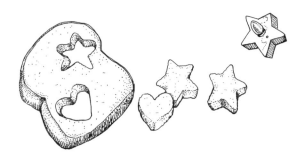

A toasty soup topping that's fun for kids! Butter bread slices and cut into shapes using mini cookie cutters. Place on a baking sheet and bake at 425 degrees for a few minutes, until crisp.

Simple Soup Suppers

Saint Basil's Soup

Marcia Shaffer
Conneaut Lake, PA

A very old recipe, handed down through many generations. It makes a simple vegetarian soup that's perfect for St. Basil's Day on January 14, at the depth of winter...or anytime, really!

6 T. oil	8 c. water
1 c. onion, sliced	2 cubes beef, chicken or
1/2 lb. sliced mushrooms	vegetarian bouillon
2 stalks celery, sliced	1 T. fresh parsley, chopped
2 carrots, peeled and sliced	salt and pepper to taste

Heat oil in a skillet over medium heat; add onion and cook until softened. Transfer onion mixture to a 4-quart slow cooker; add remaining ingredients and mix well. Cover and cook on low setting for 7 to 8 hours. Makes 4 to 6 servings.

French Onion Soup

Ed Kielar
Whitehouse, OH

This is very easy to make...homemade soup is the best!

1/2 c. butter	4 to 6 slices French bread
2 T. olive oil	4 to 6 slices Provolone cheese
4 c. onions, sliced	1-1/4 c. shredded Swiss cheese
4 10-1/2 oz. cans beef broth	1/4 c. grated Parmesan cheese
1 t. dried thyme	

Melt butter with olive oil in a large soup pot over medium heat; add onions. Cook until onions are translucent. Add beef broth and thyme; simmer over medium-low heat for 30 minutes. Meanwhile, arrange bread slices on an ungreased baking sheet. Bake at 350 degrees for 4 to 6 minutes, until toasted. To serve, ladle soup into oven-safe bowls. Top each bowl with one slice toast and one slice provolone cheese; divide Swiss and Parmesan cheeses among bowls. Broil in the oven until cheese is bubbly. Serves 4 to 6.

Mom's Best
Sunday Suppers

Minestrone Soup

Lorraine King
Lisle, IL

I always enjoy making this soup on a cold winter day. Halfway through the cooking time, you can add other vegetables like shredded cabbage, cubed zucchini, cooked carrots and peas.

4 slices bacon, cut into
1-inch pieces
1 c. onion, sliced
1/2 c. celery, chopped
10-3/4 oz. can bean &
bacon soup
10-3/4 oz. can tomato soup

14-1/2 oz. can beef broth
1-1/2 c. water
1/3 c. small elbow macaroni,
uncooked
1 t. dried basil
2 cloves garlic

Cook bacon in a Dutch oven over medium heat. Remove bacon to a plate, reserving drippings in pan. Add onion and celery to drippings; cook until onion is translucent. Add remaining ingredients, inserting a wooden toothpick through both garlic cloves. Bring to a boil. Reduce heat to medium-low; cover and simmer 25 minutes, stirring occasionally. Discard garlic and toothpick before serving. Makes 4 to 6 servings.

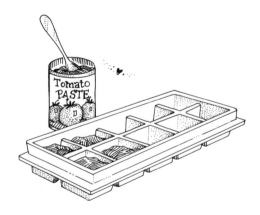

Tomato paste adds rich flavor to soups and sauces. Since many recipes only call for a tablespoon or two, save the rest of the can by spooning it into ice cube trays to freeze.

Simple Soup Suppers

Creamy Chicken Tortellini Soup

Mary Patenaude
Griswold, CT

If you're looking for an easy and delicious recipe to make with leftover roast chicken, this is it! For a thicker soup, mix 1/3 cup of cold water with 3 tablespoons cornstarch and add to soup, stirring constantly, until thickened.

1/4 c. butter
1 onion, diced
2 carrots, peeled and finely chopped or shredded
2 stalks celery, finely chopped or shredded
4 c. chicken broth

2 cubes chicken bouillon
12-oz. pkg. frozen cheese tortellini, uncooked
4 c. milk
2 c. half-and-half
4 c. cooked chicken, diced

Melt butter in a large soup pot over medium heat. Add onion, carrots and celery; sauté until tender. Add chicken broth and bouillon; bring to a boil. Add tortellini and cook for 15 minutes, or until tender, stirring occasionally. Reduce heat to low; add milk, half-and-half and chicken. Cook, stirring constantly, until heated through. Makes 6 to 8 servings.

Need just a dash of lemon or lime juice to add zest to a pot of soup? Pierce the fruit with an ice pick, squeeze out as much as needed and return it to the refrigerator until next use.

Mom's Best
Sunday Suppers

Oven Beef Stew

Elizabeth Smithson
Mayfield, KY

A woman I worked with brought in this stew one day. It was so good, I just had to have the recipe. Just the thing to simmer in the oven all Sunday afternoon...the aroma will make you want it sooner! Enjoy with cornbread, biscuits or crackers.

1 lb. stew beef cubes
1 c. onion, diced
1 to 2 T. oil
2 cloves garlic, chopped
3 14-oz. cans beef broth
4 c. tomato juice
1 c. tomato sauce
1 c. potatoes, peeled and diced

1 c. carrots, peeled and diced
1 c. celery, diced
3 cubes beef bouillon
2 t. brown sugar, packed
1 t. sugar
salt and pepper to taste
1 c. frozen green peas

In a skillet over medium heat, brown beef with onion in oil until beef cubes are browned on all sides. Add garlic; cook for one more minute. Transfer beef mixture to an ungreased large roaster pan; add remaining ingredients except peas. Cover and bake at 300 degrees for 3 to 3-1/2 hours, stirring occasionally. Stir in peas during the last 30 minutes of cooking. Makes 10 to 12 servings.

Browning adds lots of flavor to beef stew! For the very best flavor, pat the stew cubes dry with a paper towel before browning. Don't crowd the pieces in the pan, and be sure to stir up all the tasty browned bits at the bottom.

Fresh Side Dishes

Mom's Best
Sunday Suppers

Mom's Super-Simple Sunday Fruit Salad

Lynn Grundstrom
Kennedy, NY

This was my mom's special salad for Sunday dinner. She would change the ingredients to match the season, and during the holidays, she would use red grapes and green apples to make it festive. This recipe can be easily doubled.

1 T. butter
1 T. all-purpose flour
1 c. milk
1 T. sugar
1 t. vanilla extract

3 c. assorted fresh fruit such as apples, pears, raisins, bananas, dates, grapes, cut into bite-size pieces
Optional: fruit preservative

Melt butter in a saucepan over medium heat; sprinkle with flour and stir well. Gradually add milk, stirring to remove any lumps. Cook until thickened and smooth, stirring constantly. Remove pan from heat; set pan in a bowl of ice water. Stir in sugar and vanilla. Cool completely, stirring occasionally to keep sauce from forming a skin. Combine all fruit in a large bowl; add fruit preservative, if needed. Spoon cold sauce over fruit and toss to combine. Cover and chill until ready to serve. Makes 6 to 8 servings.

Bring out Mom's prettiest vintage cut-glass serving bowl when serving colorful fruit salads...they'll taste even yummier!

Fresh Side Dishes

Party Mashed Potatoes

Linda Belon
Wintersville, OH

Creamy, delicious mashed potatoes that go with all your favorite Sunday dinners! Garnish with chopped fresh chives and a big pat of butter.

5 lbs. russet potatoes, peeled and quartered	2 T. butter
salt to taste	1 t. salt
8-oz. pkg. cream cheese, softened	1/4 t. onion salt
	1/8 t. garlic salt
1 c. sour cream	1/4 t. pepper
	paprika to taste

In a large saucepan, cover potatoes with water; add salt. Boil over medium-high heat for 15 to 20 minutes, until potatoes are tender when pierced with a fork. Drain; mash potatoes until smooth. Add remaining ingredients except paprika; beat until light and fluffy. Place potatoes in a greased 2-quart casserole dish. Bake, uncovered, at 350 degrees for 30 minutes. Sprinkle with paprika; place briefly under the broiler, until golden. Makes 10 servings.

Potatoes come in 3 basic types. Starchy russet potatoes bake up fluffy and are great for frying too. Round waxy potatoes are excellent in soups, casseroles and potato salads. All-purpose potatoes are in between and work well in most recipes. Do some delicious experimenting to find your favorites!

Mom's Best
Sunday Suppers

Mom's Shoepeg Casserole
Carolyn Deckard
Bedford, IN

Looking through some of my mom's recipes, I found this one that Mom made for us kids. She always served this with pork chops or baked chicken...it was one way to get us to eat our vegetables!

15-oz. can white shoepeg
  corn, drained
14-1/2 oz. can cut green
  beans, drained
1/2 c. celery, chopped
1/2 c. green pepper, sliced
1/4 c. onion, chopped

1 c. sour cream
1/2 c. shredded sharp Cheddar
  cheese
1 sleeve round buttery crackers,
  crushed
1/2 c. margarine, melted
1/2 c. slivered almonds

Combine all vegetables and sour cream in a bowl. Mix well and transfer to a lightly greased 2-quart casserole dish. Top with cheese. Toss together crackers and melted margarine in a separate bowl; sprinkle over cheese. Top with almonds. Bake, uncovered, at 350 degrees for 20 to 25 minutes, until bubbly and golden. Makes 4 to 6 servings.

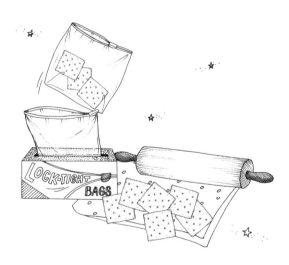

Quickly crush crackers or chips for recipes...no muss, no fuss. Simply place them in a large plastic zipping bag and crush with a rolling pin.

Fresh Side Dishes

Summary Squash Casserole
Jessica D'Ambrosio
Berlin, CT

My mom used to make this yummy casserole often when I was growing up, and now I make it for my family. It's one of my husband's favorites!

3 T. butter
1 yellow squash, halved
   lengthwise and sliced
   1/4-inch thick
1 zucchini, halved lengthwise
   and sliced 1/4-inch thick

3 T. grated or shredded
   Parmesan cheese
2 t. garlic powder
2 t. dried parsley
3 T. seasoned dry bread crumbs

In a large skillet, melt butter over medium-high heat. Add squash and zucchini; sauté until tender and lightly golden. Stir in cheese and seasonings. Transfer to a lightly greased 8"x8" baking pan; sprinkle with bread crumbs. Bake, uncovered, at 375 degrees for 15 to 20 minutes, until golden on top. Serves 4.

Lima Bean Casserole
Delma Branscome
Lynchburg, VA

We have enjoyed this recipe for years. It's easy and delicious.

10-oz. pkg. frozen lima beans
1/8 t. salt
10-3/4 oz. can Cheddar
   cheese soup

1/2 c. milk
1/2 c. celery, chopped
6-oz. can French fried onions,
   divided

Cook lima beans according to package directions, adding salt; drain. In a bowl, mix cheese soup, milk and celery; fold in beans and half of onions. Transfer to a greased one-quart casserole dish. Bake, uncovered, at 350 degrees for 20 minutes. Sprinkle with remaining onions; bake 10 more minutes. Makes 6 servings.

111

Mom's Best
Sunday Suppers

Never-Fail Scalloped Potatoes

Agnes Ward
Ontario, Canada

These scalloped potatoes are the best...this recipe never fails!

2 T. butter
3 T. all-purpose flour
1 t. salt
1/4 t. pepper
1-1/2 c. milk

1 c. shredded Cheddar cheese
1-3/4 lbs. potatoes, peeled, thinly sliced and divided
1 onion, halved and thinly sliced and divided

In a small non-stick skillet, melt butter over medium heat. Stir in flour, salt and pepper until smooth. Gradually stir in milk; bring to a boil. Cook and stir for 2 minutes; remove from heat. Add cheese and stir until blended. Arrange half of sliced potatoes in a 1-1/2 quart casserole dish coated with non-stick vegetable spray; layer with half of onion slices and half of cheese sauce. Repeat layers. Cover and bake at 350 degrees for 50 minutes, or until bubbly and potatoes are tender. Makes 6 servings.

Turn Never-Fail Scalloped Potatoes into a hearty main dish. Simply layer cubes of baked ham along with the potatoes.

Fresh Side Dishes

Green Pea Salad with Bacon & Cheese

Nancy Johnson
Laverne, OK

One of my grandmothers used to make a salad similar to this, and it was always one of my favorite salads. This has a few ingredients she didn't use, but I like the additional ingredients.

4 slices bacon
3/4 c. mayonnaise
1 T. honey
salt and pepper to taste
20-oz. pkg. frozen green
    peas, thawed

2 stalks celery, chopped
1/3 c. onion, chopped
1/2 c. shredded Cheddar cheese

Cook bacon in a skillet over medium-high heat, until crisp. Drain bacon on paper towels, reserving one tablespoon drippings. In a bowl, whisk together reserved drippings, mayonnaise, honey, salt and pepper until smooth; set aside. In a large bowl, combine crumbled bacon, peas, celery, onion and cheese. Drizzle dressing over salad and toss to coat. Cover and refrigerate until chilled, about 30 minutes. Makes 8 servings.

Serve up a salad buffet for a warm-weather Sunday dinner. Try a favorite chicken or tuna salad, a potato or pasta salad, a crisp green tossed salad and a fruity gelatin salad. Crusty bread and a simple dessert complete a tasty, light meal.

Mom's Best
Sunday Suppers

Skillet Zucchini & Tomatoes

Barbara Klein
Newburgh, IN

This is our favorite zucchini recipe. Can't wait for summer, fresh tomatoes and zucchini! I love this recipe because it is quick, easy and so very delicious, especially when you use fresh ingredients from the garden.

2 T. oil
1/2 c. onion, sliced
2 to 3 ripe tomatoes, peeled
   and quartered
1 t. salt
1/4 t. pepper
1 to 1-1/2 lbs. zucchini, peeled
   and sliced

1 bay leaf
1/2 t. basil
Garnish: grated Parmesan cheese
Optional: shredded mozzarella
   cheese

Heat oil in a large skillet over medium heat; sauté onion for 5 minutes. Stir in tomatoes, salt and pepper. Cover and simmer for 5 minutes. Stir in zucchini, bay leaf and basil; cover and simmer for 20 minutes, or until zucchini is tender. At serving time, remove bay leaf; sprinkle with Parmesan cheese. For a heartier dish, sprinkle with mozzarella cheese as well. Makes 6 servings.

Pop unripe tomatoes into a brown paper grocery bag
and store in a dark closet...they'll ripen overnight.

Fresh Side Dishes

Creamy Spinach Casserole
Eileen Steitz Watts
Cape Coral, FL

We love this recipe. It can be served as a delicious side dish for a holiday meal, a special occasion or simply for dinner.

10-oz. pkg. frozen chopped spinach
3-oz. pkg. cream cheese, softened
1/4 c. milk
1 egg, beaten
1/4 t. salt
1/4 t. pepper
Optional: 1/8 t. nutmeg
1/2 c. plain dry bread crumbs
1/4 c. grated Parmesan cheese
1 Bermuda or red onion, sliced 1/4-inch thick

Cook spinach according to package directions; drain and set aside. In a large bowl, blend cream cheese, milk, egg and seasonings. Fold in spinach, bread crumbs and cheese. Arrange onion slices in the bottom of a greased 8"x8" baking pan; top with spinach mixture. Cover with aluminum foil. Bake at 350 degrees for 35 to 40 minutes. Makes 6 servings.

Fresh greens are tasty and good for you...they're easy to mix & match in recipes too. Try spinach, kale, Swiss chard, turnip greens, broccoli rabe or peppery mustard greens, added to stir-fries or just simmered in broth with a little sautéed onion.

Mom's Best
Sunday Suppers

French Potato Salad

Joan Baker
Westland, MI

This is a recipe given to my mom by her sister-in-law back in the early 60s. My brothers don't usually like potato salad, but loved this one. This is especially good for those who don't care for mayo.

6 to 8 potatoes, peeled, cooked and cubed or sliced	2 T. cider vinegar
	2 T. onion, minced
2 T. oil	1 T. fresh parsley, minced

Make Dressing ahead of time; refrigerate. At serving time, combine all ingredients in a large bowl; mix well. Add enough dressing to coat well. Toss and serve. Makes 6 servings.

Dressing:

1/2 c. water	1/2 t. dry mustard
2 T. oil	1 egg, lightly beaten
1 T. all-purpose flour	3 T. cider vinegar
1 T. sugar	1/4 c. sour cream
1-1/2 t. salt	1/2 t. celery seed

Combine water, oil, flour, sugar, salt and mustard in the top of a double boiler. Cook over boiling water until smooth and creamy, stirring often. Whisk together egg and vinegar in a small bowl. Gradually add to cooked mixture, beating hard and consistently. Cook for 5 minutes over low heat, stirring often, until slightly thickened. Remove from heat. Stir in sour cream and celery seed. Cover and and refrigerate until ready to serve.

It's a lovely thing...everyone sitting down together, sharing food.
—Alice May Brock

Fresh Side Dishes

Fern's Pickled Beets

Debra Arch
Kewanee, IL

My mother-in-law gave me this recipe. It is very delicious and my kids love them!

3 15-oz. cans sliced beets,
   drained and 1 c. juice
   reserved
1 c. cider vinegar

1 c. sugar
1/2 t. cinnamon
1/4 t. ground cloves

Place beets in a large saucepan; set aside. In a bowl, whisk together reserved beet juice and remaining ingredients; pour over beets. Bring to a boil over medium heat; simmer for 10 minutes. Cool; transfer to a bowl. Cover and keep refrigerated. Makes 8 servings.

Fresh Cucumber Salad

Judy Scherer
Benton, MO

My great-grandmother and grandmother would pick the cucumbers from the garden to make this salad. Finally, I was able to get the recipe written down.

3 cucumbers, sliced
3/4 c. sugar
3/4 c. water

1/4 c. white vinegar
1 onion, thinly sliced

Place cucumbers in a 1-1/2 quart container with a tight-fitting lid; set aside. In a bowl, combine sugar, water and vinegar; add onion. Spoon over cucumbers and mix together. Cover and let stand for one hour and serve, or cover and refrigerate before serving. Serves 10 to 12.

Fill the sink with hot soapy water when you start dinner and just toss in pans and utensils as they're used. Clean-up will be a breeze!

Mom's Best
Sunday Suppers

Lou's Overnight Mac & Cheese
Donna Carter
Ontario, Canada

This recipe is my mother's recipe from many years ago. She has passed it down to me and it's one of my favorites. Just prep the night before and bake in the oven the next day...so easy! It's a great side dish for buffets.

10-3/4 oz. can Cheddar
   cheese soup
1 c. milk
1 c. elbow macaroni, uncooked
1/2 c. onion, chopped

1 c. shredded medium
   Cheddar cheese
1 t. garlic powder
1 t. dried parsley
1 t. dried basil

In a large bowl, whisk together soup and milk until well blended. Stir in uncooked macaroni and remaining ingredients. Transfer to a 2-quart casserole dish lightly coated with non-stick vegetable spray. Cover and refrigerate overnight. Uncover and bake at 350 degrees for 30 to 40 minutes, checking for doneness after 30 minutes. Makes 4 to 6 servings.

For hearty salads in a snap, keep unopened cans of diced tomatoes, black olives, garbanzo beans and marinated artichokes in the fridge. They'll be chilled and ready to toss with fresh greens at a moment's notice.

Fresh Side Dishes

Marinated Summer Garden Tomatoes

Ed Kielar
Whitehouse, OH

These are delicious, especially made in summertime with fresh-picked tomatoes, but can be made 'year round too with supermarket tomatoes.

6 large ripe tomatoes, cut
   into wedges
1/2 c. green onions, thinly sliced
1/3 c. olive oil or canola oil
1/4 c. red wine vinegar or
   cider vinegar

1/4 c. fresh parsley, minced
2 cloves garlic, minced
1 t. dried thyme
1 t. salt
1/4 t. coarse pepper

Combine tomatoes and onions in a shallow serving bowl; set aside. Combine remaining ingredients in another bowl; stir well and spoon over tomato mixture. Cover and refrigerate at least 2 hours. Serve with a slotted spoon. Makes 10 servings.

After a hearty Sunday dinner, serve up a Southern-style vegetable plate at suppertime. With 2 or 3 scrumptious veggie dishes and a basket of buttery cornbread, no one will even miss the meat.

Mom's Best
Sunday Suppers

Mom's Pasta Slaw

Jessica Branch
Colchester, IL

My mom used to make this slaw and I love it for outdoor gatherings in spring and summer. I use a pair of kitchen scissors to chop up the coleslaw mix.

7-oz. pkg. ditalini or small shell
  pasta, uncooked
6-oz. pkg. shredded coleslaw
  mix, finely chopped
2 stalks celery, finely chopped

1 red pepper, finely chopped
1-1/3 c. mayonnaise
1/3 c. sugar
1/4 c. cider vinegar
salt and pepper to taste

Cook pasta according to package directions. Drain in a colander; rinse with cold water and allow to cool in colander. In a large bowl, combine coleslaw mix, celery and red pepper; set aside. In a small bowl, blend together remaining ingredients except salt and pepper. Add cooked pasta to coleslaw mixture; add dressing and stir to coat well. Season with salt and pepper; cover and refrigerate until serving time. Makes 10 to 12 servings.

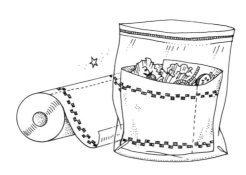

Toss together salads for several days' meals so dinner is quick & easy. Store salad greens in a plastic zipping bag, tuck in a paper towel to absorb extra moisture and refrigerate. They'll stay crisp for up to 4 days.

Fresh Side Dishes

Carrots Creole-Style

Bonnie Richards
Medford, OR

An easy and delicious side dish, made with ingredients usually found in your kitchen.

1 lb. carrots, peeled and sliced
1/8 t. salt
10-3/4 oz. can tomato soup
1/4 c. sugar
1/4 c. oil

1/4 c. white vinegar or cider vinegar
1/2 c. onion, diced
1/4 c. green pepper, diced

In a saucepan, cook carrots in salted water until tender, about 12 minutes; drain and return to pan. Meanwhile, whisk together remaining ingredients in a bowl; spoon over carrots. Heat through and serve. Makes 4 servings.

Schnitzel Beans

Kara Kimerline
Galion, OH

A family favorite made with fresh green beans. It came from an old church cookbook and I have tweaked it with peppered bacon. Sweet and savory too!

4 thick slices peppered bacon, diced
1 c. sugar
1/2 c. cider vinegar

1-1/2 lbs. fresh green beans, trimmed
1/2 c. onion, chopped

Cook bacon in a large skillet over medium heat until crisp; do not drain. Stir in sugar and vinegar; cook and stir until sugar dissolves. Add green beans and onion; simmer for 20 minutes. Serves 4 to 6.

Fussy eaters in the family? Whenever you discover a recipe they really enjoy eating, add a star in the cookbook, alongside the recipe.

Mom's Best
Sunday Suppers

Mom's Calico Salad

Wendy Ball
Battle Creek, MI

Family reunions always were fun for us children. We played with cousins, ate great food and had a turn at cranking the ice maker to make fast-melting ice cream. Mom always brought the greatest baked beans, but I always gravitated to her Calico Salad. I still make it today, with a few new tricks up my sleeve.

2 c. small shell or elbow
   macaroni, uncooked
2 T. cider vinegar
2 T. onion, grated
1 c. celery, diced
1 c. green pepper, diced
1 c. red, yellow and/or orange
   peppers, diced

1 c. grape tomatoes or assorted-
   color tomatoes, halved
1/2 c. sour cream, Greek yogurt
   or mayonnaise
2 T. chopped pimentos
Optional: diced green chiles
   to taste
salt and pepper to taste

Cook macaroni according to package directions, just until tender. Drain, reserving 1/2 cup pasta water for later; don't rinse macaroni. Place warm macaroni in a large bowl; toss with vinegar. Cover and chill overnight. Next day, combine remaining ingredients in another bowl; mix well and stir into the chilled macaroni. Cover and chill until ready to serve. If salad is too thick, stir in reserved pasta water. Makes 4 to 6 servings.

A container of sour cream will stay fresh and tasty longer
if a teaspoon or two of white vinegar is stirred in
after first opening it.

Fresh Side Dishes

My Husband's Favorite Salad

Susan Young
Mount Victory, OH

*This recipe is the result of buying too much fresh produce
at my Amish friend's vegetable stand!*

2 ears sweet corn, kernels cut off
3/4 c. sweet onion, diced
3 cucumbers, peeled and diced
3 ripe tomatoes, chopped
6-oz. can black olives, drained
1/2 lb. provolone cheese, cubed
8-oz. bottle zesty Italian salad
  dressing
salt and pepper to taste

In a large bowl, toss all ingredients together, adding salad dressing to taste. Cover and chill, or serve immediately. Makes 6 to 8 servings.

Whip up some Tangy Green Onion Dressing for a tossed salad. Blend 1/3 cup mayonnaise, 1/4 cup sour cream, one tablespoon milk, one teaspoon lemon juice and 2 finely chopped green onions. Chill to allow flavors to blend.

Mom's Best
Sunday Suppers

Southern Creamed Potato Salad

Marilyn Moseley
Oldtown, ID

This is my mother-in-law's recipe, which I have tweaked a bit through the years. It is without doubt, a family favorite! Some in our family do not enjoy onions, and so using green onions still adds a great mild flavor to the salad that all the family can enjoy.

5 lbs. russet potatoes, peeled
   and quartered
3/4 c. mayonnaise
1/2 c. Dijon mustard
1 T. dill pickle juice
1 T. salt

1 t. pepper
6 eggs, hard-boiled, peeled
   and cubed
1/4 c. green onions, diced
1/4 c. dill pickles, diced
1 T. paprika

Cover potatoes with water in a large saucepan. Cook over medium-high heat until fork-tender. Drain potatoes; add to a large bowl. Beat with an electric mixer on low to medium speed until creamy and free of lumps. Gently mix in mayonnaise, mustard, pickle juice, salt and pepper, adjusting all amounts as needed. Add eggs, onions and pickles; blend well. Smooth potatoes with a spoon; sprinkle with paprika. May immediately serve warm, or cover and refrigerate for 2 hours before serving chilled. Serves 8.

For hard-boiled eggs, use eggs that have been refrigerated at least 7 to 10 days, instead of fresher eggs…the shells will slip right off.

124

Fresh Side Dishes

Summer Bean & Corn Salad

Ronda Hauss
Bluffton, SC

This salad is a favorite at family & friend get-togethers...it's a perfect side at barbecues. I always bring a copy or two of the recipe to share. It's easily doubled or tripled.

19-3/4 oz. can black beans, drained and rinsed
11-oz. can sweet corn & diced peppers, drained
1 c. cherry or grape tomatoes, quartered
1/2 c. red onion, chopped

1 T. fresh cilantro or basil, chopped
1/2 c. ranch salad dressing
Optional: one to 2 shakes hot pepper sauce
Optional: lime wedges

In a large bowl, combine all ingredients except lime wedges; mix well. Cover and chill at least 2 hours. At serving time, garnish with lime wedges, especially if cilantro is used. Makes 6 to 8 servings.

Spoon colorful veggie salads into wide-mouth mini canning jars...convenient and fun for a summer buffet.

Mom's Best
Sunday Suppers

Tomato, Corn & Avocado Salad

*Panda Spurgin
Bella Vista, AR*

*I like to use a variety of ripe tomatoes when I make this salad.
Sometimes I add fresh herbs such as basil or oregano to the dressing.*

4 c. cherry, grape or pear
   tomatoes, halved
1 ear sweet corn, cut from cob,
   or 3/4 c. frozen corn
1 avocado, peeled, pitted
   and diced

2 green onions, thinly sliced
2 T. lime juice
1 T. olive oil
salt and pepper to taste

Combine all vegetables in a large bowl; lightly toss and set aside. Stir
together lime juice and olive oil in a cup; fold into vegetable mixture.
Season with salt and pepper. Cover and refrigerate for one hour before
serving. Makes 4 to 6 servings.

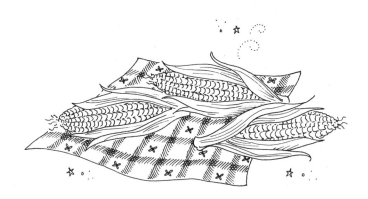

Here's an easy tip for husking sweet corn. Pull on a pair of
rubber gloves, then give each cob a quick twist between
gloved hands. The corn silk will rub right off.

Fresh Side Dishes

Cheesy Bread Pudding

Sandy Ann Ward
Anderson, IN

A forgotten dish worth remembering! So easy to make,
and great for family gatherings.

5 slices bread, crust removed
   and cubed
1-1/2 c. whole milk
1 c. shredded Cheddar cheese

3 eggs, lightly beaten
1 t. Worcestershire sauce
salt and pepper to taste

Arrange bread cubes evenly in a buttered one-quart casserole dish; set aside. Add milk to a saucepan over medium heat; bring just to a boil and remove from heat. Beat in remaining ingredients; pour mixture over bread. Allow to stand at least 15 minutes, until liquid is absorbed by bread. Bake, uncovered, at 300 degrees for 40 to 50 minutes, until firm. Cut into squares; serve warm. Serves 6 to 8.

Mother's Onion Rice

Lesa Day
Bloomfield, IN

My mother's recipe, now mine...very special! Everyone always waited
for this favorite. It's even wonderful warmed up, if there's any left
over. It's been in the family for at least 65 years.

1/2 c. margarine, melted
1-1/4 c. long-cooking rice,
   uncooked
4-oz. can sliced mushrooms

10-1/2 oz. can French onion
   soup
10-1/2 oz. can beef consommé

Spread margarine in a 2-quart casserole dish. Add uncooked rice and undrained mushrooms; pour in soups. Do not stir. Cover and bake at 350 degrees for 30 minutes; uncover and stir. Bake, uncovered, another 30 minutes. Remove from oven; cover but do not stir until serving time. Makes 8 servings.

Whip up an easy side dish! Layer thick slices of juicy tomatoes with fresh mozzarella cheese, then drizzle with olive oil.

Mom's Best
Sunday Suppers

Aunt Ted's Hominy Casserole

Beckie Apple
Grannis, AR

My husband's Aunt Thelma, lovingly called Aunt Ted, was famous for her hominy casserole. We loved her and her hominy dish.

2 15-1/2 oz. cans yellow
  hominy, drained
8-oz. container sour cream
4-oz. can chopped green chiles
2 T. onion, finely chopped
1/4 t. garlic powder

1/8 t. salt
1/8 t. pepper
1-1/2 c. shredded Cheddar
  cheese
2 slices American cheese

In a large bowl, combine all ingredients except American cheese; mix well. Spoon into a 2-quart casserole dish sprayed with non-stick vegetable spray. Bake, uncovered, at 350 degrees for 30 minutes. Lay American cheese slices on top and return to oven for another 5 minutes, or until cheese melts. Makes 6 to 8 servings.

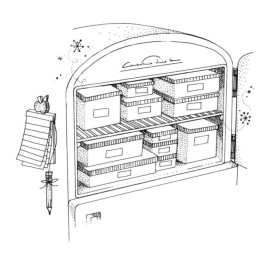

Keep a couple of favorite side dishes tucked away in the freezer. Pair with hot sandwiches or a deli roast chicken to put a hearty homestyle meal on the table in a hurry.

Fresh Side Dishes

Skillet Spanish Rice

Sherri Lopez
Albuquerque, NM

Very tasty! For a meatless dish, omit the ground beef,
and stir in 1/2 cup shredded cheese just before serving.

2 T. oil
1/2 lb. ground beef
3/4 c. onion, thinly sliced
1/2 c. green pepper, chopped
1 c. long-cooking rice, uncooked

2 8-oz. cans tomato sauce
1-3/4 c. hot water
1 t. salt
1/8 t. pepper

Heat oil in a skillet over medium heat; add beef, onion, green pepper and uncooked rice. Cook and stir until beef is lightly browned; drain well. Add remaining ingredients and mix well. Bring quickly to a boil. Reduce heat to medium-low; cover tightly and simmer for 25 minutes. Makes 4 servings.

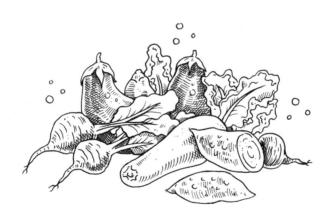

Mother always said, "Eat your veggies!" For the healthiest meals, choose from a rainbow of veggies...red beets, orange sweet potatoes, yellow summer squash, dark green kale and Brussels sprouts, purple eggplant and blueberries. Fill your plate and eat up!

Mom's Best
Sunday Suppers

Mom's Macaroni Salad

Marilyn Donovan
Fitchburg, MA

Mom made this sweet and tangy salad for us all year 'round, adding a chopped tomato whenever we had fresh tomatoes from our garden. I'm always asked to bring this to family get-togethers. It's great with burgers and hot dogs, and just as good with barbecued ribs or chicken tenders!

16-oz. pkg. elbow macaroni,
  uncooked
3 eggs, hard-boiled, peeled
  and chopped
8-oz. pkg. pasteurized process
  cheese, cubed
3 T. sugar

3 T. cider vinegar
Optional: 1 to 2 ripe tomatoes,
  chopped
19-oz. bottle mayonnaise-style
  salad dressing
salt and pepper to taste

Cook macaroni according to package directions; drain. Rinse in cold water; drain again. In a large bowl, combine macaroni, eggs and cheese; mix gently. Sprinkle with sugar and vinegar. Fold in tomatoes, if using. Add salad dressing; mix until well blended. Season with salt and pepper. Cover and chill until serving time. Serves 8 to 10.

Do you have a jar that's really hard to open? Give Mom's old trick a try...gently insert the tip of a blunt table knife under the edge of the lid. That's usually enough to break the vacuum, allowing the lid to twist right off.

Fresh Side Dishes

Edna's BLT Pasta Salad

Carolyn Deckard
Bedford, IN

I can always remember asking Mom to make this salad for my twin sister and me. We loved this salad...hope you enjoy it too.

12-oz. pkg. bowtie pasta,
  uncooked
3/4 to 1 lb. bacon, crisply cooked
  and crumbled
1/2 green pepper, diced
3 ripe tomatoes, diced
1/2 c. mayonnaise
1/2 t. salt
1/4 t. pepper
Optional: lettuce

Cook pasta according to package directions; drain. Rinse in cold water; drain again. Add bacon, green pepper, tomatoes and mayonnaise; season with salt and pepper. If making ahead, add bacon just before serving to maintain crispness. Serve in a lettuce-lined bowl, if desired. Serves 6.

Dad's Sunday Baked Fries

Gladys Kielar
Whitehouse, OH

Dad made homemade fries on Sundays. Now we use his recipe and remember him while we're enjoying the fries.

2 baking potatoes, cut lengthwise
  into thin wedges
1/4 c. grated Parmesan cheese
1/2 t. paprika
1/8 t. pepper
salt to taste

Place potato wedges in a plastic zipping bag; spray wedges with non-stick vegetable spray. Combine cheese, paprika and pepper in a cup; add to bag. Close bag and shake to coat potatoes with seasonings. Lightly spray a 15"x10" jelly-roll pan with non-stick vegetable spray. Arrange potatoes on pan in a single layer. Bake at 425 degrees for 30 minutes, or until crisp and fork-tender, turning once. Season with salt. Serves 4.

Mom's Best
Sunday Suppers

Fried Green Tomatoes with Horseradish Sauce

Jessica Kraus
Delaware, OH

Every Sunday, my grandpap would fry up some green tomatoes and everyone would gobble them up. This is my version!

4 green tomatoes, sliced
    1/4-inch thick
salt to taste
1 c. all-purpose flour
1-1/2 t. onion powder
1-1/2 t. garlic powder

4 eggs
1-1/2 c. panko bread crumbs
3/4 c. grated Parmesan cheese
1 T. Cajun seasoning
salt and pepper to taste
oil for frying

Make Horseradish Sauce ahead of time; refrigerate. Season tomato slices on both sides with salt; place on a wire rack to dry out for about 10 minutes. Set up bowls as follows. In the first bowl, combine flour, onion powder and garlic powder. Beat eggs in a second bowl; in a third bowl, combine bread crumbs, cheese and seasonings. In a heavy skillet, heat 1/4-inch oil over medium-low heat. Dredge tomatoes in flour mixture, then in egg, and then in bread crumbs. Working in batches, add tomatoes to hot oil; cook until golden on each side. Drain on paper towels. Serve with Horseradish Sauce. Serves 4.

Horseradish Sauce:

1 c. sour cream
2 T. grated horseradish,
    or to taste

2 cloves garlic, minced
2 T. lemon juice
salt and pepper to taste

Combine sour cream, horseradish, garlic and lemon juice in a small bowl. Season with salt and pepper. Cover and refrigerate to allow the flavor to develop...the longer, the better.

Fresh Side Dishes

Pea & Cauliflower Salad
Valeria Reckert-Jacobsen
Sunbright, TN

This is a family favorite that my mom would make in the summertime for family meals and get-togethers. Great flavor!

1 head cauliflower, cut into
    bite-size pieces
2/3 onion, chopped
1 c. mayonnaise
3 T. milk

1 t. seasoned salt
1/8 t. pepper
8-oz. pkg. sharp Cheddar
    cheese, cubed
12-oz. pkg. frozen peas

In a large bowl, combine all ingredients except frozen peas; mix well. Fold in peas. Cover and refrigerate for at least one hour, or for best flavor, refrigerate overnight. Serve chilled. Makes 6 to 8 servings.

If Sunday is going to be a busy day, fix a favorite make-ahead salad on Saturday night and tuck in the fridge. When Sunday dinnertime arrives, simply pull it out and serve.

Mom's Best
Sunday Suppers

Easy Caesar Pasta Salad

Danielle Boyd
Wytheville, VA

*This colorful pasta salad is especially delicious
on a hot summer day. If you can't find radiatore,
rotini is a good substitute*

16-oz. pkg. radiatore pasta,
  uncooked
2 c. cherry tomatoes, halved
1 yellow onion, peeled and diced
1 green pepper, diced

1 cucumber, peeled and diced
6-oz. pkg. finely shredded
  Parmesan cheese
16-oz. bottle classic Caesar
  salad dressing

Cook pasta according to package directions. Drain and rinse with cold water; transfer to a large bowl. Add vegetables and cheese. Drizzle with desired amount of salad dressing; toss to mix well. Serve immediately, or cover and chill until serving time. Makes 10 servings.

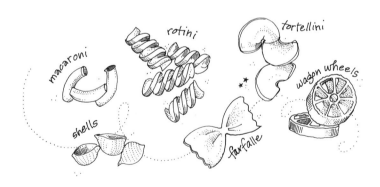

When a recipe calls for pasta, there are lots of shapes to choose from at the grocery store...why not experiment? Try using corkscrews, shells, bowties and rainbow pasta just for fun!

Fresh Side Dishes

Onion-Cheese Pie

Denise Bliss
Milton, NY

*This is a Bliss family must when serving roast beef for
Sunday dinner. It's scrumptious!*

1 sleeve buttery club crackers,
  finely crushed
1/4 c. plus 2 T. butter, melted
  and divided
1-1/2 c. onions, thinly sliced

2 eggs, lightly beaten
3/4 c. milk
salt and pepper to taste
1/4 c. shredded Cheddar cheese

In a bowl, mix cracker crumbs and 1/4 cup melted butter. Press evenly
into the bottom and up the sides of an 8" pie plate, forming a crust; set
aside. In a skillet over medium heat, sauté onions in remaining butter
until tender and golden. Spread onion mixture evenly in crust. In
another bowl, whisk together eggs, milk and seasonings; pour over
onions. Sprinkle with shredded cheese. Bake at 350 degrees for
30 minutes, or until a knife tip inserted in the center comes out clean.
Let stand for several minutes; cut into wedges. Makes 6 to 8 servings.

Fill up a relish tray with crunchy fresh veggies as
a simple side dish...add a cup of creamy salad
dressing to enjoy as a veggie dip.

Mom's Best
Sunday Suppers

Mandarin Orange Salad

Anne Ptacnik
Holdrege, NE

This salad recipe is a keeper. My mom used to make it often for family gatherings, and everyone always loved it, even the kids! The sugared almonds take it to the next level and give it a great crunch.

1/2 c. sliced almonds
3 T. sugar
1/2 head iceberg lettuce, torn
1/2 head romaine lettuce or fresh spinach, torn

1 c. celery, chopped
Optional: 2 green onions, chopped
11-oz. can mandarin oranges, chilled and drained

Prepare Dressing ahead of time; cover and chill. In a small saucepan over medium heat, cook almonds with sugar, stirring constantly until almonds are coated and sugar is dissolved and lightly golden. Watch closely, as it burns easily. Set aside to cool. At serving time, combine lettuces, celery, onions if using, oranges and almonds. Top with dressing and toss well. Makes 4 to 6 servings.

Dressing:

1/4 c. oil
2 T. sugar
2 T. vinegar
1 T. fresh parsley, chopped

1/2 t. salt
1/8 t. pepper
1/8 t. hot pepper sauce

Whisk together all ingredients; cover and chill until serving time.

Sprinkle a tossed green salad with ruby-red pomegranate seeds for a festive touch.

Fresh Side Dishes

Mom's Cheesy Corn Casserole
Kylee Lenhart
Sylvania, OH

This dish is a must-have for all of our holiday meals! We always beg my mom to make this, because she does it best.

3 15-1/2 oz. cans corn, drained
10-3/4 oz. can can cream of
   celery soup
1 c. sour cream
1/2 c. onion, chopped

1 c. shredded Cheddar cheese
1 sleeve round buttery crackers,
   crumbled
1/2 c. butter, melted

In a large bowl, combine all ingredients except crackers and butter; mix well. Transfer to a lightly greased 9"x9" baking pan. In another bowl, combine cracker crumbs and melted butter; sprinkle on top. Bake, uncovered, at 325 degrees for 30 to 40 minutes, until bubbly and golden. Makes 6 servings.

Lucy's German Potato Salad
Barbara Klein
Newburgh, IN

My 96-year-old mom makes this delicious salad for every summer gathering. Mom has 7 children, 18 grandchildren and 22 great-grandchildren. We are blessed!

6 potatoes
2 or more slices bacon, diced
1/4 c. onion, chopped
1/4 c. green pepper, diced
salt and pepper to taste
2 T. all-purpose flour

1 c. cider vinegar
1 c. sugar
2 t. celery seed
1 t. mustard
Garnish: 2 eggs, hard-boiled,
   peeled and sliced

In a saucepan, cover unpeeled potatoes with water; cook over high heat until fork-tender. Drain; peel potatoes and slice. Meanwhile, cook bacon in a skillet over medium heat until crisp. Remove bacon from skillet; reserve drippings. In a large bowl, combine potatoes, bacon, onion, green pepper, salt and pepper; set aside. In same skillet over medium heat, stir flour into reserved drippings; add vinegar, sugar, celery seed and mustard. Bring to a boil; cook until slightly thickened. Mix with potatoes; serve slightly warm, or cover and refrigerate. Garnish with sliced eggs and serve. Serves 6 to 8.

Cheesy Ranch Hashbrowns

Karen Wilson
Defiance, OH

Everyone loves cheesy potatoes! With the addition of ranch dressing, they're even better.

30-oz. pkg. frozen shredded potatoes, thawed
8 slices bacon, crisply cooked and crumbled
8-oz. pkg. cream cheese, room temperature
1 c. sour cream
1/4 c. butter, melted
1-oz. pkg. ranch salad dressing mix
8-oz. pkg. shredded Cheddar cheese, divided

Combine all ingredients in a large bowl, reserving one cup Cheddar cheese for topping. Mix well; spread evenly in a greased 1-1/2 quart casserole dish. Cover with aluminum foil. Bake at 350 degrees for one hour. Remove foil; top with remaining cheese and bake an additional 10 minutes, or until melted. Makes 8 servings.

Mmm...is anything better than bacon? To separate bacon slices easily, first let the package stand at room temperature for about 20 minutes.

Fresh Side Dishes

Perfectly Parmesan Potatoes

Irene Robinson
Cincinnati, OH

This tasty casserole can be assembled the night before,
covered and refrigerated until time to bake.

32-oz. pkg. frozen diced
   potatoes, thawed
3 c. half-and-half

1/2 c. butter, sliced
1/2 t. salt
1/2 c. grated Parmesan cheese

Spread potatoes in a greased 13"x9" baking pan; set aside. In a saucepan over medium-low heat, combine half-and-half, butter and salt; heat through. Spoon hot mixture over potatoes; sprinkle with cheese. Bake, uncovered, at 350 degrees for one hour. Makes 6 servings.

Tressie's Coleslaw

Ruth Harmeling
Louisville, KY

This is my husband's favorite slaw recipe. It came from
my great-grandmother, Tressie.

4 c. cabbage, shredded
3/4 c. mayonnaise
1/4 c. oil

5 T. cider vinegar
3 T. sugar
1 t. celery seed

Place cabbage in a large bowl; set aside. Combine remaining ingredients in a jar; cover and shake to combine well. Pour over cabbage; toss to mix well. Cover and chill at least 3 hours. Toss again and serve. Makes 10 servings.

Make a flavorful drizzle for steamed veggies. In a saucepan, simmer 1/2 cup balsamic vinegar, stirring often, until thickened. So simple and scrumptious.

Mom's Best
Sunday Suppers

Zucchini Slaw

Teresa Eller
Kansas City, KS

I love all kinds of slaws! They go with everything from casseroles to sandwiches. This one is a favorite.

2 c. zucchini, thinly sliced
1 c. yellow crookneck squash, thinly sliced
1 c. green or purple cabbage, thinly sliced
1 c. carrots, peeled and thinly sliced

1 c. green onions, thinly sliced
1 c. celery, thinly sliced
1/2 c. olive oil
1/4 c. cider vinegar
zest and juice of 1 lemon
1 t. dill weed

Combine all vegetables in a large bowl; set aside. In a separate bowl, whisk together remaining ingredients; pour over vegetable mixture. Toss to mix well; cover and refrigerate overnight. At serving time, if slaw is too wet, drain off some of the liquid; if too dry, add a small amount of oil and vinegar or lemon juice. Makes 6 to 8 servings.

For a quick and casual centerpiece, fill a vintage egg basket with a variety of colorful vegetables.

Fresh Side Dishes

Cannellini & Broccolini Salad
Sharon Tillman
Hampton, VA

This salad of beans and greens is tasty and refreshing. My grandson just likes to say the name! Sometimes I'll add chopped cherry tomatoes or roasted red peppers for color. If you can't find broccolini, just cut broccoli into bite-size pieces. Enjoy!

1 lb. broccolini, trimmed
1 t. salt
3 T. olive oil
1 t. lemon zest
2 T. lemon juice
2 T. honey mustard

2 T. capers, drained
1/2 t. red pepper flakes
salt and pepper to taste
15-1/2 oz. can cannellini beans,
   drained and rinsed

Add broccolini and salt to a large saucepan of boiling water over medium-high heat. Cook for one to 2 minutes, until crisp-tender. Drain; rinse with cold water and pat dry. Cut broccolini into bite-size pieces; set aside. In a bowl, combine remaining ingredients except beans; whisk well. Add broccolini and beans; toss to coat. Cover and chill until serving time. Makes 6 servings.

It's not how much we have, but how much we enjoy,
that makes happiness.
–Charles Haddon-Spurgeon

Mom's Best
Sunday Suppers

Strawberry-Onion Salad

Linda Diepholz
Lakeville, MN

This is a wonderful salad to serve when juicy strawberries are in season. The salad can be assembled ahead of time, but do not add the dressing until ready to serve.

1 bunch romaine lettuce, torn
1/2 c. red onion, thinly sliced

2 c. fresh strawberries, hulled
and sliced

In a large bowl, toss lettuce, onion and strawberries; set aside. Drizzle Poppy Seed Dressing over lettuce mixture; toss lightly. Serve immediately. Makes 6 servings.

Poppy Seed Dressing:

1 c. mayonnaise-style salad
dressing or mayonnaise
1/3 c. sugar

1/4 c. milk
2 T. cider vinegar
1 T. poppy seed

Combine all ingredients in a small bowl; mix well.

Use a large plastic drinking straw to hull strawberries with ease. Just push the straw through the end without a stem and the green, leafy top will pop right off!

Fresh Side Dishes

Frosted Fruit Salad

Shannon Reents
Poland, OH

This is a recipe my mom made often back in the 80s. She gave me the recipe to carry on!

3-oz. pkg. lemon gelatin mix
3-oz. pkg. orange gelatin mix
2 c. boiling water
1-1/2 c. cold water
11-oz. can crushed pineapple,
   drained and juice reserved

2 bananas, sliced
1-1/2 c. mini marshmallows
2 T. all-purpose flour
1/2 c. sugar
1 egg, beaten

In a large bowl, combine gelatin mixes and boiling water; stir until dissolved. Stir in cold water. Cover and refrigerate until gelatin begins to set. Add pineapple, banana slices and marshmallows; stir well. Transfer to an 8"x8" glass baking pan; cover and chill until firm. Meanwhile, in a small saucepan, combine flour, sugar, egg and reserved pineapple juice. Cook over low heat until thickened, stirring constantly. Cool; spread over firm gelatin. Cover and chill until serving time; cut into squares. Makes 8 to 10 servings.

Try Mom's old trick for coring a head of iceberg lettuce easily. Hold the lettuce with the core facing the kitchen counter. Bring it down hard on the counter...the core will loosen and can be pulled right out with your fingertips.

Mom's Best
Sunday Suppers

Mom-Mom Anne's Noodle Kugel

Cindy Slawski
Medford Lakes, NJ

My grandmother brought this recipe came to the United States from Russia when she was a teenager. My whole family loves it. I think of my grandmother and mother every time we eat it. I usually serve it warm the first day, and then have some cold for breakfast the next day...either way, it will taste great!

12-oz. pkg. wide egg noodles,
  uncooked
1 c. cottage cheese
1/2 c. sour cream
1 egg, beaten
1/2 c. sugar, or more to taste

1/2 c. raisins, rinsed and
  patted dry
1/2 t. cinnamon
1/2 c. butter, sliced
Optional: additional cinnamon

Cook noodles according to package directions; drain and transfer to a bowl. Add cottage cheese, sour cream, egg, sugar, raisins and cinnamon; mix well. Press into a buttered deep 2-quart casserole dish or 13"x9" baking pan. Dot with butter; top with a little cinnamon, if desired. Bake, uncovered, at 375 degrees for about 1-1/2 hours, until set and golden. Serve warm or chilled. Makes 8 to 10 servings.

For plump, juicy raisins, cover them with boiling water or apple juice and let stand for 15 minutes. Drain and pat dry with a paper towel before adding to the recipe.

Fresh Side Dishes

Barb's Deviled Eggs

Barbara Klein
Newburgh, IN

My family loves this recipe for deviled eggs! I make them for all family gatherings. I have to hide them before serving time, so that everyone gets a chance to have one.

1 doz. eggs, hard-boiled, peeled
   and halved
1/2 c. mayonnaise-style salad
   dressing
1 T. mustard

salt to taste
8 green olives with pimentos,
   chopped, or to taste
Garnish: paprika

Scoop out egg yolks and add to a bowl, setting aside egg white halves. Mash egg yolks with a fork; stir in salad dressing, mustard and salt, adding more dressing if a creamier consistency is desired. Fold in olives. Spoon egg yolk mixture into egg whites. Sprinkle with paprika; cover and chill until serving time. Makes 2 dozen.

Maggie's Quick Pickles

Emilie Britton
New Bremen, OH

This recipe came from my sister Maggie. It's a longtime family favorite, especially in the summertime when the cucumbers and onions are fresh from the garden!

8 c. cucumbers, sliced
2 c. onions, sliced
1 T. salt
2 c. sugar

1-1/2 c. white vinegar
2 t. celery seed
2 t. mustard seed

Combine cucumbers and onions in a large bowl; sprinkle with salt and toss to coat. Let stand for one hour. In another bowl, combine sugar, vinegar, celery seed and mustard seed; stir until sugar is dissolved. Drain cucumbers and transfer to a non-metallic container. Pour vinegar mixture over cucumbers. Cover and chill at least 24 hours to blend flavors. Serves 8 to 10.

Mom's Best
Sunday Suppers

Spinach Salad with Eggs & Bacon

Sandy Ann Ward
Anderson, IN

This is a wonderful salad for a formal dinner or gathering. Since the dressing is made the night before, save time by cooking the eggs and bacon then too. At serving time, toss and serve.

4 eggs, hard-boiled, peeled and sliced or quartered
8 slices bacon, crisply cooked and crumbled
10-oz. pkg. fresh spinach, torn
1 c. sliced mushrooms
1 red onion, thinly sliced
Garnish: salad croutons

Make Spinach Salad Dressing the night before; refrigerate. Shortly before serving time, combine all ingredients in a large bowl. Drizzle with desired amount of dressing and serve. Makes 6 servings.

Spinach Salad Dressing:

1/2 c. olive oil
1/2 c. red wine vinegar
3 T. catsup
1/4 c. sugar
1/2 t. garlic powder
1/2 t. dry mustard
1 t. salt
1 t. pepper

Combine all ingredients in a lidded jar. Cover jar; shake well. Refrigerate overnight before serving; shake well before using.

If there's leftover salad after dinner, use it for a tasty sandwich filling the next day. Split a pita round, stuff with salad and drizzle with salad dressing...yummy!

Pass the Bread, Please

Mom's Best
Sunday Suppers

Yeast Dinner Rolls

Stephanie Schultz
Galena, MD

I always make these rolls to serve with Sunday dinner pot roasts and holiday dinners. I've perfected the recipe over the years, and they're always requested when I bring a dish to a family gathering. I hope you enjoy them, too!

2 T. active dry yeast
1 c. plus 2 T. very warm water,
   110 to 115 degrees
1/3 c. oil
1/4 c. sugar

1 egg, beaten
1/2 t. salt
3-1/2 c. bread flour, divided
3 T. butter, melted

In a large bowl, combine yeast, warm water, oil and sugar. Stir to combine. Let stand for 15 minutes, or until yeast foams and puffs up. Stir in egg and salt. Add 2 cups flour; beat with an electric mixer on low speed, using a dough hook. Beat in remaining flour, 1/2 cup at a time. Mix until dough pulls from the sides of the bowl and forms into a ball. Divide dough into 12 pieces. Roll dough into balls, using your hands. Place balls on a large parchment paper-lined baking sheet; allow to rise for 30 minutes, or until almost double in size. Bake at 400 degrees for 9 to 10 minutes, just until tops of rolls are barely golden. Remove from oven and brush melted butter over tops of rolls. Return to oven; bake for 5 more minutes, or until tops are deeply golden. Makes one dozen.

Happiness is like jam. You can't spread even a little
without getting some on yourself.
–Unknown

Pass the Bread, Please

Tried & True Honey Oat Bread
Miranda Ching
Kaneohe, HI

What's better on a cool day than freshly baked bread? This is our family's regular sandwich bread. Though it takes awhile, there's not much "hands-on" effort to this recipe...the bread machine does most (or all) of the work. Though I like to bake it in a bread pan in the oven, it can be baked right in your bread machine, too. Just follow the manufacturer's instructions.

1-1/3 c. warm water, 100 to 110 degrees
3 T. coconut oil or canola oil
3 T. honey
1 t. salt
2 c. all-purpose or bread flour

1-1/2 c. regular or white whole-wheat flour
1/2 c. old-fashioned rolled oats, uncooked
1 env. active dry yeast

Add all ingredients to bread machine pan, in order recommended by bread machine manual. Set to dough cycle. When cycle is done, remove dough to a greased surface. Punch down dough and roll up into a log. Place dough into a well-greased 9"x5" loaf pan. Cover with a damp tea towel; let rise for 25 to 30 minutes. Uncover and bake at 375 degrees for 35 minutes, or until dark golden on top. Turn out immediately onto a wire rack. Let cool completely; wrap and store. Makes one loaf.

A new way to enjoy quick bread! Cut into thick slices and butter both sides. Grill or broil until golden and toasted. Sprinkle with powdered sugar and serve with jam.

Mom's Best
Sunday Suppers

Apple Spice Muffins

Judy Henfey
Cibolo, TX

This was one of the first muffin recipes I learned to bake when I was first married, 35 years ago. Simple and delicious... and your house will smell great!

1-1/2 c. all-purpose flour
2 t. baking powder
1/2 t. salt
1/4 t. nutmeg
1-1/2 t. cinnamon, divided
1 egg, beaten

1/2 c. milk
1/4 c. oil
3/4 c. sugar, divided
1/2 t. vanilla extract
1 c. apples, peeled, cored
   and diced

In a bowl, whisk together flour, baking powder, salt, nutmeg and 1/2 teaspoon cinnamon; set aside. In a separate bowl, beat together egg, milk, oil, 1/2 cup sugar and vanilla; slowly stir in flour mixture. Fold in apples. Divide batter among 12 greased or paper-lined muffin cups, filling 2/3 full. Combine remaining sugar and cinnamon; sprinkle evenly over muffins. Bake at 400 degrees for 20 to 25 minutes; cool on a wire rack. Makes one dozen.

Let someone know you think they're the best! Tie a blue ribbon around a loaf of bread or a basket of muffins. Add a tag that says "Blue-Ribbon Friend!"

Pass the Bread, Please

Beckie's Corn Muffins

Beckie Apple
Grannis, AR

*I serve these tasty corn muffins with soups,
stews and chili...my family loves them!*

1 c. self-rising flour
1/2 c. yellow cornmeal
2 T. baking powder
1/4 c. sugar
2/3 c. milk

1/4 c. oil
1 egg, beaten
1/2 c. shredded Cheddar cheese
1 c. corn, well drained

In a large bowl, combine flour, cornmeal, baking powder and sugar; mix well. Add remaining ingredients and mix well. Generously coat 12 muffin cups with non-stick vegetable spray; add batter, filling 2/3 full. Bake at 400 degrees for 20 minutes, or until golden. Makes one dozen.

Mom's Mexican Bread

Barbara Imler
Noblesville, IN

My mother gave me this recipe, which was an unusual one for her because she didn't care for spicy foods. These bread slices aren't too spicy, though, just enough to be tasty. Delicious with Mexican food!

1 thin loaf French bread, cut into
1/2-inch slices
1 c. butter, room temperature
1 c. canned diced green chiles,
drained

1 clove garlic, minced
1 c. mayonnaise
2 c. shredded Monterey Jack or
taco-blend cheese

Place bread slices on a baking sheet and broil until toasted on one side. In a bowl, blend butter, chiles and garlic. Spread on the untoasted sides of bread. In another bowl, mix mayonnaise and cheese; spread over butter mixture. Broil until cheese is puffy and golden, watching closely to avoid burning. Serves 6 to 8.

To peel garlic easily, crush the clove with the side of a knife.

151

Mom's Best
Sunday Suppers

No-Fail Potato Rolls

Linda Wilcoxon
Nokesville, VA

I have been making these rolls more years than I can remember. They have wonderful flavor and keep well. I also use them in place of store-bought rolls for glazed party sandwich recipes and they take those recipes to new heights! They are wonderful for gift-giving...turn them out of the round cake pan together for a pretty presentation. You will not be disappointed!

2 envs. instant rapid-rise yeast
1-1/3 c. very warm water,
   110 to 115 degrees, divided
2/3 c. shortening
2/3 c. sugar
1 c. mashed potatoes

2 eggs, beaten
2-1/2 t. salt
6 to 6-1/2 c. all-purpose flour,
   divided
Garnish: melted butter

In a small bowl, dissolve yeast in 2/3 cup warm water. In a large bowl, blend shortening and sugar; stir in potatoes, eggs and salt. Add dissolved yeast to shortening mixture. With an electric mixer on medium speed, beat in 2 cups flour and remaining warm water. Stir in enough of remaining flour to form a soft dough. Shape dough into a ball; do not knead. Place in a greased bowl, turning once to grease top of dough. Cover with a tea towel and let rise in a warm place until double in size, about one hour. Punch down dough and divide into 3 portions. Shape each portion into 13 to 15 balls; arrange in 3 greased 9" round cake pans. Cover and let rise until double, 30 minutes to one hour. Uncover and bake at 350 degrees for 20 to 25 minutes, until golden. Remove from oven; brush butter over tops. Let cool in pans for 10 to 12 minutes. Carefully remove rolls to a wire rack to cool, keeping rolls together. Makes about 3-1/2 dozen.

Such sweet placecards...tie a ribbon around each guest's stemmed glass and tuck in a tiny childhood snapshot.

Pass the Bread, Please

Fresh Herb Butter

Vickie
Gooseberry Patch

Warm, fresh-baked bread deserves special butter, and this is it! This flavorful butter is scrumptious on pasta and veggies, too.

1 c. butter, softened
1 T. shallot, finely chopped
2 t. fresh parsley, chopped

1 t. fresh thyme, chopped
1 t. lemon zest
1/2 t. garlic, minced

Combine all ingredients in a small bowl; mix together with a fork. Cover and refrigerate at least one hour, to allow flavors to blend. Makes about one cup.

If you've bought a bunch of fresh herbs for a recipe that calls for just a couple of tablespoons, freeze the rest! Chop the extra herbs and spoon into an ice cube tray, one tablespoon per cube. Cover with water and freeze. Frozen cubes can be dropped right into hot stew or soup.

Mom's Best
Sunday Suppers

Dilly Casserole Bread

Pam Crane
Morganton, GA

This is a recipe I got from Mom...I'm not sure where she got it from. It is my "comfort bread." Try it, and you'll love it too!

1 env. active dry yeast	1 egg
1/4 c. very warm water,	2 t. dill seed
110 to 115 degrees	1 t. salt
1 c. cottage cheese, heated to	1/4 t. baking soda
lukewarm	2-1/4 to 2-1/2 c. flour, divided
2 T. sugar	Garnish: softened butter, salt
1 T. butter	to taste

In a small bowl, soften yeast in warm water. In a large bowl, combine warm cottage cheese, softened yeast and remaining ingredients except flour and garnish. With an electric mixer on low speed, beat in one cup flour. On medium speed, gradually beat in enough of remaining flour to form a stiff dough. Cover with a tea towel. Let rise in a warm place for 50 to 60 minutes, until light and double in size. Stir down dough; turn into a well-greased 1-1/2 to 2-quart round casserole dish. Let rise in a warm place for 30 to 40 minutes, until light. Bake at 350 degrees for 40 to 50 minutes, until golden. Brush with soft butter; sprinkle with salt. Makes one loaf.

Keep fresh-baked bread warm and toasty! Tuck a piece of aluminum foil into a bread basket and top it with a decorative tea towel. Add the bread and flip the ends of the towel over it.

Pass the Bread, Please

Simple & Delicious Dinner Rolls

Kathleen Sturm
Corona, CA

This is my go-to dinner roll recipe. It is great for the bread basket at dinner, and also for making sandwiches. Pillow-soft and buttery... you couldn't ask for a better dinner roll! Very simple to make using a bread machine.

1 c. very warm water,
   110 to 115 degrees
2 T. butter
1 egg, beaten
3-1/4 c. bread flour

1/4 c. sugar
1 t. salt
3 t. instant yeast
Garnish: additional butter,
   softened

Add all ingredients except garnish to bread machine pan in the order listed, or according to your bread machine's directions. Choose the dough cycle. When the dough cycle is complete, divide dough into 12 equal balls; roll into balls using your hands. Arrange dough balls in a greased 13"x9" baking pan. Cover with a tea towel; let rise in a warm place until double, about 45 minutes. Uncover and bake at 375 degrees for 12 to 15 minutes, until golden. Remove from oven; immediately brush with additional softened butter. Makes one dozen.

Sweet little servings of butter for a festive table are oh-so easy to make. Press softened butter into decorative candy molds, then chill and pop out.

Mom's Best
Sunday Suppers

Mom's Biscuits

Rosemary Trezza
Winter Springs, FL

My mom was famous in our family for her biscuits. When we were kids in school, Mom would bake these biscuits to have ready when we came home. We loved them hot from the oven, with lots of butter on them. We would all be gathered around the kitchen table. I can still hear Mom saying, "The biscuits are rich enough without butter!" Mom would turn her back (on purpose, of course), and our Nana (who lived with us) would motion for us to put some butter on the biscuits. Many days, our aunt and cousins (who lived next door) would come over to enjoy these biscuits too. For the adults, put on the coffee, and for us kids, get out the milk. Those were wonderful days and memories I will never forget!

2 c. all-purpose flour
4 t. baking powder
1 t. salt

4 to 5 T. shortening
3/4 c. plus 1 T. whipping cream, divided

In a large bowl, combine flour, baking powder and salt; mix well. Cut in shortening with a spatula. Mix in 3/4 cup cream until a soft dough forms; shape into a ball. Knead dough several times on a floured surface; divide into 2 parts. Roll one ball into a thin cylinder, 3/4-inch thick. Cut into 1/2-inch slices and place on a greased baking sheet. Repeat with second ball of dough. Brush tops of biscuits with remaining cream. Bake on center rack of oven at 425 degrees for 15 minutes, or until lightly golden; if not done, bake for another 5 minutes. Makes one dozen.

Making biscuits and there's no biscuit cutter handy?
Try Mom's little trick...just grab a glass tumbler or
the open end of a clean, empty soup can.

Pass the Bread, Please

Apricot Freezer Jam

Carrie O'Shea
Marina Del Rey, CA

When we first moved to California, we were delighted to find apricot trees in our backyard. We've been trying out apricot recipes ever since...this one is a real keeper!

2-1/2 c. ripe apricots, halved, pitted and chopped
2 T. lemon juice
5-1/2 c. sugar
3/4 c. water
5 T. powdered fruit pectin
6 1/2-pint plastic freezer jars with lids, sterilized

Combine apricots and lemon juice in a bowl. Add sugar and stir well; set aside for 10 minutes. In a small saucepan over medium-high heat, stir together water and pectin. Cook and stir to a full rolling boil; boil hard for one minute. Add pectin mixture to apricot mixture; stir for 3 minutes. Spoon jam into jars, leaving 1/2-inch headspace; wipe tops and secure lids. Refrigerate until set. Keep refrigerated up to 3 weeks, or freeze up to one year. Makes about 6, 1/2-pint jars.

Cinnamon Honey Butter

Teresa Verell
Roanoke, VA

This makes a special treat to share with family & friends.

1/2 c. butter, softened
1/4 c. honey
2 t. powdered sugar
1/2 t. cinnamon
1/4 t. nutmeg

Combine all ingredients in a bowl. Beat with an electric mixer on low speed until blended; beat on medium speed to a spreading consistency. Transfer to a crock; cover and refrigerate. Makes 3/4 cup.

Streusel-Topped Blueberry Muffins

Mary Lou Thomas
Portland, ME

The streusel topping is optional to add, but really...
why wouldn't you? It's scrumptious!

1-3/4 c. all-purpose flour
1/3 c. sugar
2 t. baking powder
1/4 t. salt
1 egg, beaten

3/4 c. milk
1/4 c. oil
3/4 c. fresh or frozen blueberries
1 t. lemon zest, finely shredded

In a large bowl, combine flour, sugar, baking powder and salt. Make a well in center of flour mixture; set aside. In another bowl, whisk together egg, milk, and oil. Add egg mixture all at once to flour mixture. Fold in blueberries and lemon zest. Stir just until moistened; batter should be lumpy. Spoon batter into 12 greased or paper-lined muffin cups, filling each 2/3 full. Sprinkle Streusel Topping over batter. Bake at 400 degrees for 18 to 20 minutes, until a toothpick comes out clean. Set pan on a wire rack for 5 minutes. Remove from muffin cups; serve warm. Makes one dozen.

Streusel Topping:

3 T. all-purpose flour
3 T. butter

2 T. chopped pecans or walnuts

Stir together flour and butter until mixture resembles coarse crumbs. Stir in nuts.

Berries won't sink to the bottom if you toss them with
a tablespoon of flour before adding to the batter.

Pass the Bread, Please

Amish White Bread

Rhonda Reeder
Ellicott City, MD

When I was visiting farmers' markets in Amish country, a sweet lady shared this easy recipe with me. My family loves it! It slices and toasts well, so it's good for breakfast. Add sugar to your own preference, as this is a sweet bread.

1/3 to 2/3 c. sugar
2 c. very warm water, 110 to
    115 degrees
1-1/2 T. active dry yeast

1/4 c. oil
1-1/2 t. salt
6 c. bread flour

In a large bowl, dissolve sugar in warm water; stir in yeast. Let stand for several minutes, until mixture is foamy. Add oil and salt to yeast mixture; stir well. Stir in flour, one cup at a time. Knead dough on a lightly floured surface until smooth. Place dough in a well-greased bowl, turning dough to coat. Cover with a damp tea towel. Allow to rise for about one hour, until double in bulk. Punch dough down; knead for a few minutes. Divide dough in half and shape into 2 loaves. Place in 2 well-greased 9"x5" loaf pans. Let rise for 30 minutes, or until dough has risen one inch above pans. Bake at 350 degrees for 30 minutes, or until golden. Makes 2 loaves.

Are you baking yeast bread from scratch? A convenient place to let the dough rise is inside your microwave. Heat a mug of water on high for 2 minutes. Then remove the mug, place the covered bowl of dough inside and close the door.

Mom's Best
Sunday Suppers

Sun-Dried Tomato Bread
Kathy De Schinckel
Davenport, IA

This bread is easy to make and delicious with homemade soups! The Parmesan Butter makes it even better.

2-1/2 c. all-purpose flour
1/3 c. plus 2 T. grated Parmesan
  cheese, divided
1 T. sugar
2 t. dried, minced onions
1 t. baking soda
1 t. dried basil

1/2 t. salt
1 c. sour cream
1/3 c. milk
1/3 c. sun-dried tomatoes in oil,
  drained and chopped
1/4 c. butter, melted
1 egg white, lightly beaten

Make Parmesan Butter; set aside or refrigerate. In a large bowl, mix together flour, 1/3 cup Parmesan cheese, sugar, onions, baking soda, basil and salt. Stir in sour cream, milk, tomatoes and melted butter just until moistened. Turn dough onto a lightly floured surface and knead about 10 times, until smooth. Divide dough in half. Pat each half into a 4-1/2 inch inch round loaf. Place loaves on a greased baking sheet, 3 inches apart. Brush tops with egg white; sprinkle with remaining cheese. Cut an X in the top of each loaf, about 1/2-inch deep. Bake at 350 degrees for 30 to 35 minutes, until golden. Remove from baking sheet; cool completely. Serve with Parmesan Butter. Makes 2 loaves.

Parmesan Butter:

1/2 c. butter, softened
2 T. grated Parmesan cheese

1 t. Italian seasoning

Combine all ingredients in a small bowl. Beat with an electric mixer on low speed until creamy. Makes about 1/2 cup.

Kindness is never wasted.
−S.H. Simmons

Pass the Bread, Please

Garden Bruschetta

Virginia Craven
Denton, TX

*We love this with our favorite pasta meals. It's a great way to use
an overabundance of ripe tomatoes of any size...fresh basil, too.*

1-1/2 c. ripe tomatoes, diced
20 to 24 fresh basil leaves,
  stacked and diced
2 to 3 T. olive oil, divided

salt and pepper to taste
1 to 1-1/2 T. balsamic vinegar
4 to 6 slices hearty rustic bread,
  1-inch thick

Combine tomatoes and basil in a bowl. Add just enough olive oil to
moisten; stir. Cover and refrigerate for 10 to 15 minutes. Season with
salt and pepper; stir in balsamic vinegar. Brush both sides of bread slices
generously with remaining oil. Add to a hot skillet over medium-high
heat; toast until golden and crusty on both sides. Spoon tomato mixture
onto bread; serve warm. Makes 6 servings.

Lemon & Chive Butter

Hope Davenport
Portland, TX

*This butter is delicious on fresh-baked bread...on potatoes,
vegetables and even broiled fish, too!*

1/2 c. butter, softened
1/4 c. fresh chives, chopped

2 T. lemon zest

Blend all ingredients in a small bowl. Shape into logs; wrap and chill.
For holiday shapes, press into cookie cutters and chill; push out butter
and serve. Makes about 3/4 cup.

For the freshest-tasting butter, keep just one stick in the fridge
at a time, and tuck the rest of the package into the freezer.

Mom's Best
Sunday Suppers

Family-Favorite Focaccia Bread
Sara Tatham
Plymouth, NH

My granddaughters practically inhale this special bread! It is truly special, with a fabulous flavor and texture. It's especially nice with an Italian meal like spaghetti or lasagna...it's great with chili or soup too.

3/4 c. plus 3 T. warm water,
   100 to 110 degrees
3 T. olive oil, divided
3 T. sugar
2 T. powdered milk
1-1/2 t. salt

3 c. all-purpose flour
2-1/4 t. active dry yeast
3 T. grated Parmesan or
   Romano cheese
3/4 t. Italian seasoning
garlic powder to taste

To bread machine pan, add warm water, one tablespoon olive oil, sugar, milk, salt, flour and yeast in the order recommended by bread machine manual. Select dough setting. When cycle is completed, turn dough onto a lightly floured surface. Cover dough and let rest for 15 minutes. Knead dough for one minute. Press dough evenly into a well-greased 15"x10" jelly-roll pan and 1/4 inch up the sides of pan. Cover and let rise in a warm place for 20 to 30 minutes, until dough is slightly risen. With a wooden spoon handle, make indentations in dough, one inch apart. Brush dough with remaining oil; sprinkle with cheese and seasonings. Bake at 400 degrees for 13 to 15 minutes, until lightly golden. Cool slightly; cut into squares and serve warm. Makes 8 servings.

Be sure to use the type of yeast a recipe calls for. Active dry yeast is usually activated with hot water before adding to a recipe, while instant dry yeast can be added straight from the package. Both types can be wrapped and stored in the freezer up to a year.

Pass the Bread, Please

Sweet Thin Skillet Cornbread

Sandra Parker
Glen Burnie, MD

*My mother made her yummy, sweet "thin" cornbread any day
of the week. This is how I remember it, with my added
touch of some Pepper Jack cheese!*

1/4 c. butter
1/2 c. yellow cornmeal
1/2 c. all-purpose flour
1/4 c. sugar
1-1/2 t. baking powder
1/4 t. salt

1/2 t. cracked pepper
2/3 c. whole milk
1 egg, beaten
1/2 c. plus 1 T. shredded Pepper
Jack cheese

Preheat oven to 425 degrees; add butter to a cast-iron skillet and
place in oven until melted. In a bowl, stir together cornmeal, flour,
sugar, baking powder, salt and pepper. Add milk, egg, cheese and
2 tablespoons melted butter from skillet, leaving remaining butter in
skillet. Stir just until combined; pour batter into hot skillet. Bake at
425 degrees for 12 to 14 minutes. Cut into wedges. Serves 6.

Cornmeal comes in yellow, white and even blue...the choice
is up to you! Stone-ground cornmeal is more nutritious
than regular cornmeal, but does have a shorter shelf life.

163

Mom's Best
Sunday Suppers

Cranberry-Walnut Muffins

Judith Smith
Bellevue, WA

I received this recipe from my aunt about 30 years ago.
I have enjoyed making the muffins throughout the years.

2 c. all-purpose flour
3/4 c. sugar
1 T. baking powder
1/2 t. baking soda
1/2 t. salt
1-1/2 c. fresh cranberries,
   chopped

1/2 c. chopped walnuts
2 eggs, beaten
1 c. milk
1/4 c. butter, softened
1 t. vanilla extract

In a large bowl, combine flour, sugar, baking powder, baking soda, salt, cranberries and walnuts. Stir well to blend; set aside. In another bowl, whisk together remaining ingredients; add all at once to flour mixture. Stir just until all ingredients are moistened. Spoon batter into 12 well-greased muffin cups, filling 2/3 full. Bake at 375 degrees for 20 to 25 minutes, until tops spring back when lightly touched. Remove from muffin pan and cool. Makes about one dozen.

Use an old-fashioned ice cream scoop to fill muffin cups
with batter. No spills, no drips and the muffins
turn out perfectly sized!

Pass the Bread, Please

6-Week Bran Muffins

Rosemary Lightbown
Wakefield, RI

My mother-in-law always made these delicious muffins. Simple to make, and everyone loved them! You can keep the batter in the fridge for up to 6 weeks. But I prefer to bake them all at once and pop the extras in the freezer, then reheat when I want to serve them.

4 eggs, beaten
1 c. oil
4 c. buttermilk
2-1/2 c. sugar

5 c. all-purpose flour
5 t. baking soda
15-oz. pkg. bran & raisin cereal
1 c. chopped dates

Mix all ingredients in a large bowl. Spoon batter into greased muffin cups, filling 2/3 full. Bake at 350 degrees for 20 to 25 minutes. Set pan on a wire rack to cool. Makes 5 dozen.

Root Beer Rye Bread

Margaret Welder
Madrid, IA

I found this recipe in a book in the 1960s and made it over & over. My kids and husband loved it. Now, it is a Christmas specialty. It is easy to do with a mixer.

2-1/2 c. root beer, heated to
    110 to 115 degrees
2 envs. instant dry yeast
1/3 c. dark or sorghum molasses
1 T. salt

1-1/2 c. rye flour
4-3/4 to 5-1/4 c. all-purpose
    flour, divided
1/4 c. butter, softened

Pour warm root beer into a large bowl; add yeast and stir until dissolved. Add molasses, salt, rye flour and 2 cups all-purpose flour; beat with an electric mixer on medium speed until smooth. Add butter; beat again. Add just enough of remaining flour to make a kneadable dough. Turn dough out onto a floured surface; knead for 5 minutes, or until smooth and flexible. Place in a large greased bowl. Cover with a tea towel; let rise until double. Punch down dough; let rest for 15 minutes. Divide dough in half; shape each into a loaf. Place in 2 greased 9"x5" loaf pans. Cover and let rise until double. Bake at 350 degrees for 45 minutes. Makes 2 loaves.

Mom's Best
Sunday Suppers

Lisa's Italian-Seasoned Flatbread

Lisa Ann Panzino DiNunzio
Vineland, NJ

This delicious flatbread is super-easy to make, with no yeast needed. You may want to double the recipe, because they'll go quick. Perfect as a side for pasta, soup, salad or just about anything...enjoy!

2 c. all-purpose flour
1 T. baking powder
2 T. grated Parmesan cheese
1 t. salt
1/2 t. garlic powder
1/2 t. onion powder
1/2 t. dried oregano
1 T. extra-virgin olive oil
1 to 1-1/4 c. warm water,
    100 to 110 degrees, divided
additional oil for frying

In a large bowl, mix together flour, baking powder, cheese, salt and seasonings. Stir in oil and one cup warm water; add remaining water, a little at a time, until dough has the consistency of pizza dough. Knead on a floured surface for 2 to 3 minutes; form into a ball. Place dough in a greased bowl; let rest for 30 minutes. Divide dough into 6 pieces. Place pieces, one at a time, between 2 pieces of parchment paper; roll out dough to 1/4-inch thickness. Heat a skillet over medium-high heat; add a very little oil to just slightly coat the bottom of pan. Fry each flatbread until golden spots form; flip and cook other side until done. Serve warm or cooled; may also freeze. Makes 6 flatbreads.

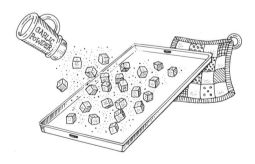

Turn leftover bread into tasty salad croutons. Toss bread cubes with olive oil, garlic powder and dried herbs. Scatter on a baking sheet and bake at 400 degrees for 5 to 10 minutes, until golden and toasty.

Pass the Bread, Please

Cheesy French Bread

Paulette Walters
Newfoundland, Canada

One of my favorites...we love this bread! It's almost like
a cheese fondue without the fondue pot.

2 T. butter
1 T. all-purpose flour
1/2 c. milk
1 egg, lightly beaten
2 T. dry white wine or water
2-1/2 c. shredded Monterey
    Jack cheese

3/4 t. garlic, finely chopped
1/4 t. nutmeg
1/8 t. cayenne pepper, or to taste
1 loaf French bread

Melt butter in a small saucepan over medium heat. Stir in flour and milk with a wire whisk; cook and stir rapidly until slightly thickened. Let cool; transfer to a bowl. Add remaining ingredients except bread; blend with a fork and set aside. Slice bread loaf down the center and cut into individual slices, halfway through loaf. Open up loaf; spoon in cheese mixture. Wrap in aluminum foil and place on a baking sheet. Bake at 300 degrees for 15 to 20 minutes, until cheese has melted, checking occasionally to avoid burning. Slice and serve warm. Serves 6.

Serve saucy pasta dishes in wide-rimmed soup plates...
there's room to set a slice of bread on the plate's rim.

Mom's Best
Sunday Suppers

Pineapple Date Loaf

Shirley Howie
Foxboro, MA

This is an old recipe that my mother used to make for us, many years ago. It is moist and very flavorful! Substitute pecans for the walnuts, if you prefer.

1/4 c. butter, softened
1/2 c. sugar
1 egg, beaten
1/4 t. lemon extract
8-oz. can crushed pineapple,
    drained and liquid reserved
1/4 c. chopped walnuts
2-1/2 c. all-purpose flour

2-1/2 t. baking powder
1/4 t. baking soda
1 t. salt
1/2 c. chopped dates
1/4 c. water
1/4 c. maraschino cherries, well
    drained and chopped

In a bowl, blend butter and sugar; blend in egg and extract. Fold in drained pineapple and walnuts; set aside. In another bowl, combine flour, baking powder, baking soda and salt; add dates and mix well. Stir flour mixture into butter mixture alternately with water and reserved pineapple juice. Fold in cherries. Pour batter into a greased 9"x5" loaf pan. Bake at 375 degrees for about 55 minutes, until a toothpick comes out clean. Cool in pan for 10 minutes; remove loaf from pan and cool completely on a wire rack. Makes one loaf.

Fresh-baked, cooled bread freezes beautifully. Wrap it in plastic, then in aluminum foil and freeze for up to 3 weeks. Add a ribbon bow for a hostess gift that's sure to be appreciated.

Pass the Bread, Please

Grandma Truda's Zucchini Bread

Monica Britt
Fairdale, WV

I had the privilege of growing up next door to my grandparents. They always grew a garden, which I loved. When the zucchini was harvested, Grandma and I would make zucchini bread together. It made the whole house smell delicious! Mix it up and add some extra ingredients, like chocolate chips, flaked coconut, raisins or dates.

3/4 c. oil
3 eggs, beaten
2 c. sugar
2 t. vanilla extract

2 c. zucchini, grated
1 T. cinnamon
3 c. self-rising flour
1 c. chopped pecans

Combine oil, eggs, sugar, vanilla and zucchini in a large bowl. Blend in cinnamon and flour; fold in pecans. Divide batter between 2 greased 9"x5" loaf pans. Bake at 325 degrees for 1-1/2 hours. Cool in pans for 10 minutes; remove loaves from pan and cool completely on a wire rack. Makes 2 loaves.

No self-rising flour in the pantry? Try this! For each cup needed, combine one cup all-purpose flour, 1-1/2 teaspoons baking powder and 1/2 teaspoon salt.

Mom's Best
Sunday Suppers

Grand-Aunt's Grecian Bread
Sheena Abbey
Nova Scotia, Canada

This is a favorite family recipe handed down from our Grand-Aunt Clara Tompkins. She made it for years, along with other breads. It is extremely easy, just ten minutes to prep and ten minutes to knead. The dough is also perfect for cinnamon rolls and pizza dough. My brother leaves the dough in the fridge overnight before rolling it out the next day for pizza. A nice addition is shredded Cheddar cheese when adding the flour.

2 c. very warm water,
   110 to 115 degrees
2 T. sugar
1-1/2 T. active dry yeast

1/4 c. olive oil
1 t. salt
5 c. all-purpose flour

Combine warm water, sugar and yeast in a large bowl; stir well and let stand for 10 minutes. Stir in oil and salt. Add flour; mix and knead until bubbly, about 10 minutes. Let rise for 45 minutes, or as long as yeast package instructions indicate. Punch down dough; cut in half and shape each half into a long loaf. Place loaves on a greased or parchment paper-lined baking sheet; cover with a tea towel. Let rise for 45 minutes. Bake at 400 degrees for 20 minutes. Cool loaves on a wire rack. Makes 2 loaves.

For a tasty change from bread & butter, serve slices of warm Italian bread with dipping oil. Pour a thin layer of extra-virgin olive oil into saucers, drizzle with a little balsamic vinegar and sprinkle with dried oregano. Scrumptious and so easy to do!

Pass the Bread, Please

Cheddar Beer Rolls

Jackie Smulski
Lyons, IL

You'll love these easy, tasty rolls. For even more flavor, you can add a variety of dried herbs, coarse pepper or Dijon mustard.

2 c. biscuit baking mix
1 c. regular or non-alcoholic beer
2 t. sugar

1 c. shredded sharp Cheddar
   cheese

Combine all ingredients in a large bowl; mix well. Spoon batter into 12 muffin cups coated with non-stick vegetable spray, filling 2/3 full. Bake at 400 degrees for 15 to 17 minutes, until golden. Cool in pan for 5 minutes. Serve warm. Makes one dozen.

Quick Rolls

Sandy Ann Ward
Anderson, IN

Something fast, easy and delicious for the bread basket on your Sunday dinner table!

2 c. self-rising flour
2 T. sugar
2 T. mayonnaise

1 c. milk
2 T. butter, diced

In a large bowl, sift flour and sugar together. Mix in remaining ingredients except butter. Spoon batter into greased muffin cups, filling 2/3 full; top each roll with a small pat of butter. Bake at 450 degrees for 10 to 15 minutes, until golden. Makes one dozen.

Add snipped fresh herbs such as dill weed, basil or thyme to biscuit dough for delicious variety.

171

Mom's Best
Sunday Suppers

Old-Fashioned Icebox Yeast Rolls

Janis Parr
Ontario, Canada

Nothing smells more heavenly than these rolls baking in the oven.

1 env. active dry yeast	1/3 c. sugar
1/4 c. very warm water,	1/2 c. cold water
110 to 115 degrees	1/2 t. salt
1/2 c. boiling water	1 egg, beaten
1/3 c. shortening	3-3/4 c. all-purpose flour

In a small bowl, combine yeast and warm water; let stand for 5 minutes. In a large bowl, pour boiling water over shortening and sugar; stir to combine. Stir in yeast mixture, cold water, salt and egg; add flour and knead until smooth. Cover and refrigerate overnight. Form dough into golf ball-size balls; place in a greased 13"x9" baking pan. Cover and let rise in a warm place until double in size. Uncover and bake at 400 degrees for 12 to 14 minutes, until golden. Makes 2 dozen.

Making yeast bread? Sprinkle a few drops of the hot water on your forearm...if it doesn't feel too hot or too cold, it's just the right temperature for dissolving yeast.

Pass the Bread, Please

Lemon Cream Biscuits

Paula Marchesi
Auburn, PA

Quick & easy to make...you'll love serving these. The less you handle the biscuits while making them, the better they'll be. They are simply delicious, great with most meals.

2 c. all-purpose flour
3 T. sugar
1 T. baking powder
1/2 t. coarse salt
2 t. lemon zest

1-1/2 c. whipping cream,
or more as needed
Garnish: butter, honey, jam
or jelly

In a large bowl, whisk together flour, sugar, baking powder, salt and lemon zest. Add cream; stir gently with a rubber spatula until just moistened. Turn dough out onto a lightly floured surface and press together with your hands, very slowly adding more cream if needed to get dough to hold together. Roll or pat dough into a circle, 3/4-inch thick. Cut into 2 to 3-inch rounds with a biscuit cutter. Place biscuits on a parchment paper-lined or lightly greased baking sheet, slightly separated. Bake at 425 degrees for 15 minutes, or until lightly golden. Serve warm, garnished as desired. Makes 1-1/2 dozen.

A well-loved china teapot that's been handed down to you makes a sweet vase for garden roses, daffodils or daisies.

Mom's Best
Sunday Suppers

Beer Mustard Biscuits

Bethi Hendrickson
Danville, PA

These biscuits are wonderful with soup and salad.
This recipe was shared with me years ago.

2 c. all-purpose flour
2 t. baking powder
1/2 t. salt
1/4 c. regular or butter-flavored
   shortening, chilled
1/4 c. butter, chilled

1/2 c. regular or non-alcoholic
   beer, chilled
1 T. plus 1-1/2 t. mustard,
   divided
1-1/2 T. milk, chilled

In a large bowl, combine flour, baking powder and salt. Cut in shortening and butter with a knife until mixture resembles coarse crumbs; set aside. In a small bowl, combine beer and one tablespoon mustard; stir into crumb mixture, just until blended. Turn out onto a floured surface; knead 8 times. Roll out dough to 1/2-inch thickness. Cut out biscuits with a 2" round biscuit cutter. Re-roll scraps and cut out additional biscuits until all dough is used. Arrange biscuits on a parchment paper-lined baking sheet, 1-1/2 inches apart. Combine remaining mustard with milk; brush over tops of biscuits. Bake at 425 degrees for 13 to 15 minutes, until lightly golden. Makes one dozen.

Make a double batch of your favorite comfort food and invite neighbors over for supper...what a great way to get to know them better. Keep it simple with a tossed salad, warm rolls and apple crisp for dessert. It's all about food and fellowship!

Pass the Bread, Please

Cheesy Cheddar Twists

Liz Blackstone
Racine, WI

Yum! These cheesy, twisty bread rings are perfect for munching alongside bowls of soup. Let the kids help make them!

2 8-oz. tubes refrigerated crescent rolls	1 egg, beaten
	1 t. water
1-1/2 c. shredded Cheddar cheese	2 t. sesame seed
	1/2 t. garlic powder
1/4 c. green onions, chopped	1/4 t. dried parsley

Separate each tube of crescent rolls into 4 rectangles, making 8 rectangles total. Press seams to seal and set aside. In a bowl, combine cheese and onions. Spoon 3 rounded tablespoonfuls of cheese mixture lengthwise down the center of each rectangle, leaving 1/4-inch at each end uncovered. Fold rectangles in half lengthwise; firmly press edges to seal. Twist each strip 4 to 5 times. Bring ends together to form a ring; pinch to seal. Place on a greased baking sheet. In a cup, whisk together egg and water; brush over rings. Combine sesame seed and seasonings; sprinkle over rings. Bake at 375 degrees for 14 to 16 minutes, until golden. Remove to wire racks; cool slightly and serve. Makes 8 rolls.

Call it a clan, call it a network, call it a tribe, call it a family:
Whatever you call it, whoever you are, you need one.
– Jane Howard

Mom's Best
Sunday Suppers

Double-Quick Dinner Rolls

Denise Burks
Ore City, TX

*Hot rolls for dinner...what a treat! These rolls are
very easy to make and do not require a lot of time.*

2-1/4 all-purpose flour, divided
2 t. sugar
1 t. salt
1 env. active dry yeast
1 c. very warm water,
    110 to 115 degrees

2 t. shortening
1 egg, beaten
Garnish: melted butter

In a large bowl, mix 1-1/4 cups flour, sugar, salt and yeast. Add warm water, shortening, and egg; mix with a fork until smooth. Stir in remaining flour until smooth. Cover with a tea towel; let rise for about 30 minutes. Stir batter down; spoon into 12 greased muffin cups. Set pan on top of stove; let rise about for 20 minutes. Bake at 350 degrees for 15 to 20 minutes, until golden. Drizzle melted butter over hot rolls. Makes one dozen.

Mix up some zesty oil & vinegar salad dressing to toss with crisp lettuce and juicy tomatoes. In a small jar, combine 3/4 cup olive oil, 1/4 cup white wine vinegar, 3/4 teaspoon salt and 1/4 teaspoon pepper. Add some minced garlic, if you like. Screw on the lid and shake well. Keep refrigerated.

Pass the Bread, Please

Old-Fashioned Garlic Bread

Kathy Grashoff
Fort Wayne, IN

*Warm and savory...a must-have with spaghetti &
meatballs, lasagna and other Italian favorites.*

1/2 c. butter, softened
1 t. garlic powder
1/2 t. salt

1 loaf Italian bread, cut in
   half lengthwise
1 T. grated Parmesan cheese

In a small bowl, combine butter and seasonings; blend well. Spread
over cut sides of bread; sprinkle with cheese. Reassemble loaf and wrap
tightly in aluminum foil; place on a baking sheet. Bake at 400 degrees
for 25 to 30 minutes, until loaf is crusty and heated through. Remove
foil; slice and serve. Serves 6 to 8.

Herb Garden Butter

Jennie Gist
Gooseberry Patch

Take a stroll through your garden and whip up something tasty!

1 c. butter, room temperature
1 t. fresh marjoram, chopped
1 t. fresh basil, chopped

1 t. fresh tarragon, chopped
1 t. fresh chives, chopped
1 t. fresh rosemary, chopped

Combine all ingredients in a small bowl; blend well. Transfer to a
covered bowl and refrigerate. Makes one cup.

When whisking ingredients in a mixing bowl, a damp
kitchen towel can keep the bowl in place. Just twist
the towel securely around the base of the bowl.

Mom's Best
Sunday Suppers

30-Minute Apple Butter

Pam Hooley
LaGrange, IN

This is a good recipe to have on hand when you're needing something special to add to a meal. You may already have the ingredients on hand!

2 c. unsweetened applesauce
1/4 c. sugar
1 t. cinnamon

1/4 t. allspice
1/8 t. ground ginger
1/8 t. ground cloves

Stir together all ingredients in a saucepan over medium-high heat; bring to a boil. Reduce heat to low and simmer for 30 minutes, stirring occasionally. Cool and serve. Makes about 1-1/4 cups.

Strawberry Microwave Jam

Donna Riley
Browns Summit, NC

You'll love serving homemade biscuits with your very own jam.

4 c. ripe strawberries, hulled and
  sliced or quartered
2 T. fresh lemon juice
1/3 to 1/2 c. sugar

1/8 t. salt
Optional: 1 t. lemon zest
2 1/2-pint canning jars with lids,
  sterilized

Place berries in a large microwave-safe bowl, filling no more than 1/3 full. Add remaining ingredients; mix well. Microwave for 5 minutes and stir. Microwave for 5 more minutes and stir. If fruit seems too chunky, microwave for another 5 minutes. Transfer jam to jars; wipe rims and add lids. Refrigerate for up to 4 weeks, or freeze for longer storage. Makes about 2, 1/2-pint jars.

For a special hostess gift, wrap up a jar of homemade jam in a lacy vintage handkerchief and tie it with a ribbon.

Pass the Bread, Please

Gram's Angel Biscuits

Sandy Coffey
Cincinnati, OH

Made for all the angels in my family. This dough can be mixed up, then kept in the fridge for several weeks and baked as needed.

5 c. all-purpose flour	1 t. salt
3 T. sugar	3/4 c. shortening
1 T. baking powder	2 c. buttermilk
1 t. baking soda	1 env. active dry yeast

In a large bowl, sift together flour, sugar, baking powder, baking soda and salt. Cut in shortening with a knife until well mixed. Add buttermilk and yeast; stir until flour is moistened. Cover and refrigerate, if not using immediately. Roll out dough on a floured surface, 1/2-inch thick; cut into biscuits with a biscuit cutter. Place on a greased baking sheet. Bake at 350 degrees for 20 minutes, or until golden. Makes about one dozen.

Mamma Char's Buttermilk Biscuits

LaDeana Cooper
Batavia, OH

Such a delicious and fluffy biscuit. When I was young, I always liked standing on a chair and "squishing" the dough together.

1 c. butter	1/2 to 1 c. buttermilk
3 c. self-rising flour	1/4 to 1/2 c. butter, melted

In a large bowl, cut butter into flour until mixture resembles coarse meal. Gradually stir in buttermilk, just until dough forms; dough will be sticky. Turn dough out onto a floured surface; fold over, 15 to 20 times. Roll out dough one to 1-1/2 inches thick. Cut out into rounds; arrange in a greased 13"x9" baking pan. Brush tops with melted butter. Bake at 350 degrees for 20 minutes, or until lightly golden. Makes about one dozen.

Mom's Best
Sunday Suppers

Grandma's Best Banana-Walnut Bread

Theresa Eldridge
Festus, MO

My grandmothers and mother were the best cooks ever. They showed their love for their family & friends by making delicious meals and treats to share. It is amazing how the smell of this bread baking in the oven fills the mind and heart with fond memories. Insanely delicious... it makes wonderful French toast too. Bake some memories with your family today!

3 to 4 ripe bananas
1/3 c. butter, melted
3/4 c. sugar
1 egg, beaten
1-1/2 t. vanilla extract
1 t. baking powder
1 t. baking soda

1/2 t. cinnamon
1/4 t. salt
1-1/2 c. all-purpose flour
1 c. chopped walnuts, chocolate
   chips or butterscotch chips
Optional: additional nuts or chips
   for topping

In a large bowl, mash bananas with a potato masher; stir in melted butter. Add sugar, egg and vanilla; stir well with a large wooden spoon. Sprinkle with baking powder, baking soda, cinnamon and salt; stir to combine. Add flour and walnuts, chocolate chips or butterscotch chips; stir just until no streaks of flour remain. Pour batter into a greased and floured 8-1/2"x4-1/2" loaf pan. If desired, sprinkle with additional nuts or chips. Bake at 350 degrees for 50 to 60 minutes, until a knife tip inserted in the center comes out clean. Cool in pan for 10 minutes; turn out onto a wire rack and cool completely. Slice into 10 thick slices and serve. Makes 10 servings.

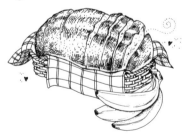

Take time to share family stories and traditions with your kids over the dinner table. A cherished family recipe can be a super conversation starter.

Treats from Mom's Kitchen

Mom's Best
Sunday Suppers

Aunt Eula's Oatmeal Pie

Carolyn Deckard
Bedford, IN

Almost every Sunday, we gathered around Grandma Hale's kitchen table to try one of Aunt Eula's new recipes that she'd brought. This oatmeal pie was one of them. Every time I make it, what great memories come back!

3 eggs	1/2 c. brown sugar, packed
1 c. light corn syrup	1/2 c. chopped walnuts or pecans
1/4 c. butter, melted	2 T. all-purpose flour
1 c. old-fashioned oats,	2 t. vanilla extract
uncooked	9-inch deep-dish pie crust,
3/4 c. flaked coconut	unbaked

In a large bowl, beat eggs with a whisk. Add remaining ingredients except crust; mix well with a spoon. Pour mixture into crust. Bake at 350 degrees for 40 minutes; increase heat to 375 degrees and bake for 10 minutes more. Cool; cut into wedges. Makes 6 servings.

Eggs work best in baking recipes when they're brought to room temperature first. If time is short, just slip the eggs carefully into a bowl of lukewarm water and let stand for 15 minutes...they'll warm right up.

Treats from Mom's Kitchen

Perfect Peach Cobbler

Becky Bosen
Layton, UT

We grow peaches in our backyard and love this recipe. Canned, well-drained peaches work also. Tastes like summer!

3 c. ripe peaches, peeled, pitted
   and sliced
1/2 c. plus 2 T. brown sugar,
   packed and divided
1/2 c. sugar
1 c. all-purpose flour

1 t. baking powder
1/8 t. salt
1 egg, beaten
6 T. butter, melted
Garnish: vanilla ice cream or
   whipped cream

Arrange peaches in a lightly greased 13"x9" baking pan; sprinkle with 2 tablespoons brown sugar and set aside. In a bowl, stir together remaining brown sugar, sugar, flour, baking powder and salt. Add egg; mix until crumbly. Sprinkle mixture over peaches; drizzle with melted butter. Bake at 350 degrees for 35 to 40 minutes. Serve warm, topped with ice cream or whipped cream. Makes 8 servings.

Fresh whipped cream is a must with Mom's best desserts, and it's simple to make. Combine one cup heavy cream with 1/4 cup powdered sugar and one teaspoon vanilla extract in a chilled bowl. Beat with chilled beaters until stiff peaks form.

Citrus Delight Bundt Cake

*Tena Huckleby
Morristown, TN*

This is my own recipe that I created myself. Whenever I serve this refreshing cake, everyone seems to enjoy it! Sprinkle the icing with additional orange and lemon zest, if you wish.

18-1/2 oz. pkg. lemon cake mix
3.3-oz. pkg. instant lemon
    pudding mix
2 eggs, beaten
1 c. orange juice
1/2 c. oil

1 t. orange extract
1/2 t. lemon zest
1/2 t. orange zest
Optional: 1 c. peanuts, coarsely
    chopped

Combine all ingredients in a large bowl. Beat with an electric mixer on medium speed for 2 minutes, or until well blended. Coat a Bundt® pan with butter-flavored non-stick vegetable spray; pour batter into pan. Bake at 350 degrees for 36 minutes, or until a toothpick comes out clean. Cool cake in pan for 10 minutes. Gently turn cake out of pan onto a serving plate; cool completely. Spread Icing over cake. Makes 10 to 12 servings.

Icing:

1/2 c. cream cheese, softened
3/4 c. powdered sugar

1/2 t. lemon zest
4 t. milk

Combine all ingredients; stir together until smooth.

Garnish desserts with a lemon twist. Cut thin slices of lemon with a paring knife, then cut from center to rind. Hold edges and twist in opposite directions...fancy!

Treats from Mom's Kitchen

Mom's Bread Pudding

Jennifer Salberg
Helendale, CA

My mom used to make this for Dad and me when I was growing up. I love bread pudding, but this is the only recipe I have ever found that comes out in a pudding consistency, with a luscious caramely sauce. Everyone likes it! The amount of bread you use makes the pudding thicker or thinner.

1 c. dark brown sugar, packed
4 to 6 slices white bread
3 to 4 T. butter, softened
1 c. raisins

2 c. milk
3 eggs, lightly beaten
1/8 t. salt
1 t. vanilla extract

Add brown sugar to the top of a double boiler. Spread bread generously with butter and tear into small pieces. Add bread to pan over brown sugar; add raisins and set aside. In a bowl, whisk together remaining ingredients; pour over bread mixture. Do not stir now or at any time during cooking. Bring water in bottom of double boiler to a boil; reduce heat to medium. Cover and simmer for one hour. To serve, spoon warm bread pudding into dishes; spoon sauce from bottom of pan over pudding. Best served warm. Makes 4 to 6 servings.

Dig into Mom's or Grandma's recipe box for that extra-special dessert you remember...and then bake some to share with the whole family.

Mom's Best
Sunday Suppers

Coconut-Pecan Squares

Patricia Harris
Hendersonville, TN

Years ago, my husband's stepmom served these tasty morsels to the family as well on sweet trays for neighbors. I always found myself stepping back to the table and having another sample. Since then, I've prepared them each year and have shared them with our neighbors too.

1/2 c. butter, softened
1/2 c. dark brown sugar, packed
1 c. plus 2 T. all-purpose flour, divided
2 eggs

1 c. light brown sugar, packed
1 c. chopped pecans
1/2 c. shredded coconut
1 t. vanilla extract
1/8 t. salt
Garnish: powdered sugar

In a bowl, blend butter and dark brown sugar. Add one cup flour; mix well. Press into a lightly greased 8"x8" baking pan, spreading batter evenly into corners. Bake at 350 degrees for 20 minutes. Meanwhile, in another bowl, beat eggs until frothy. Gradually add light brown sugar and beat until thick. Add pecans; toss coconut with remaining flour and add to bowl. Add vanilla and salt; mix well. Spread over baked crust. Bake at 350 degrees for 22 minutes, or until dark golden and solid in the center. Cool; sprinkle with powdered sugar. Cut into one-inch squares. Makes 3 dozen.

Turn a tried & true cake recipe into cupcakes...so pretty to serve, such fun to eat! Fill greased muffin cups 2/3 full of cake batter. Bake at 350 degrees until a toothpick tests clean, about 18 to 20 minutes. Cool and frost.

Treats from Mom's Kitchen

Aunt Roxie's Sugar Cookies

Beckie Apple
Grannis, AR

Growing up, I have such fond memories of my Aunt Roxie. Visiting her always meant homemade cookies. I remember watching her make my favorite sugar cookies in a crock bowl...and then, of course, the fun part that I was allowed to help with, using the cookie cutters. I am reminded of that sweet aroma of the fresh-baked cookies. I am happy to share my version of her sugar cookies!

4 c. self-rising flour	1/4 c. oil
3 c. sugar	1 egg, beaten
1/8 t. salt	1 T. milk
1/4 c. margarine, softened	1 T. vanilla extract

In a large bowl, combine flour, sugar and salt; mix thoroughly. Add remaining ingredients and stir well. Cover and chill for one hour. Divide dough into 3 equal portions. On a floured surface, roll out each portion of dough to 1/8-inch thickness. Sprinkle dough with small amounts of additional flour, as needed. Cut dough with cookie cutters into desired shapes; place cookies on parchment paper-lined baking sheets. Bake at 325 degrees for 8 to 10 minutes, until lightly golden. Let cool on pan for 5 minutes; remove to a wire rack and cool completely. Store in an airtight container. Makes 4 dozen.

When rolling out cookie dough, sprinkle the table with powdered sugar instead of flour. Tastier than using flour and it works just as well!

Mom's Best
Sunday Suppers

Poppy's Sour Cream Apple Pie

Denise Schwenger
Port Republic, NJ

After I got married, my husband's Uncle Poppy would come once a week with all kinds of delicious desserts he'd made. This was my very favorite. If it weren't for him, I wouldn't have learned to bake!

3/4 c. sugar
1 c. sour cream
2 t. all-purpose flour
1/8 t. salt
1/4 t. nutmeg

1 t. vanilla extract
2 c. apples, peeled, cored
   and diced
9-inch pie crust, unbaked

In a large bowl, combine all ingredients except apples and pie crust; beat until smooth. Fold in apples; spoon mixture into pie crust. Bake at 400 degrees for 15 minutes. Turn oven down to 350 degrees; bake for another 30 minutes. Remove from oven; add Topping and bake another 10 minutes. Cool; cut into wedges. Serves 6 to 8.

Topping:

1/4 c. butter
1 egg, beaten
1/3 c. sugar

1/3 c. all-purpose flour
1 t. cinnamon

Mix together all ingredients until crumbly.

Sprinkle a little fresh lemon juice over sliced apples before baking...the tart juice will bring out the flavor of the apples.

Treats from Mom's Kitchen

Fresh Fruit Kuchen

Joanne Wilson
Roselle Park, NJ

I first had this dessert at a family gathering when I was a teen. A neighbor brought it to the barbecue. I loved it and asked her for the recipe. Been making it ever since...always a big hit!

2 c. all-purpose flour
1 c. butter, softened
3/4 c. plus 2 T. sugar, divided
1/2 t. baking powder
1/2 t. salt
2 c. apples, pears or peaches,
    peeled, cored or pitted and
    sliced 1/4-inch thick

1 t. cinnamon
2 egg yolks, beaten
1 c. whipping cream
Garnish: whipped cream or
    vanilla ice cream

In a large bowl, mix together flour, butter, 2 tablespoons sugar, baking powder and salt until crumbly. Press into the bottom and sides of a 12"x9" baking pan coated with non-stick vegetable spray. Arrange fruit slices evenly in crust. Combine remaining sugar and cinnamon in a cup; sprinkle evenly over fruit. Bake at 400 degrees for 15 minutes. Remove from oven; reduce oven to 350 degrees. In another bowl, beat together egg yolks and cream; pour evenly over fruit. Bake at 350 degrees for 30 minutes. Remove from oven; let cool. Cover and refrigerate until serving time. Cut into squares; serve topped with whipped cream or ice cream. Makes 8 to 10 servings.

Invite family & friends to a Sunday afternoon dessert social! Everyone brings a pie, a cake or another favorite dessert... you provide the ice cream and whipped topping.

Peach-Blueberry Crumble

JoAnn
Gooseberry Patch

Serve in your favorite sundae cups, topped with a scoop
of vanilla ice cream...yummy!

4 c. ripe peaches, peeled, pitted
    and sliced
1 c. blueberries
3/4 c. sugar, divided
2 T. cornstarch
1 c. quick-cooking oats,
    uncooked

1/2 c. brown sugar, packed
1 egg, beaten
1/4 c. butter, sliced
1/4 t. cinnamon
1/4 t. nutmeg

In an ungreased 2-quart casserole dish, gently toss together fruit,
1/2 cup sugar and cornstarch; set aside. Combine remaining ingredients
in a small bowl. Stir with a fork until crumbly; sprinkle over fruit
mixture. Bake at 375 degrees for 20 to 35 minutes, until topping is
golden. Serve warm. Serves 6 to 8.

Baking together is a fun family activity for kids just beginning
to learn to cook. As you measure and mix together, be sure to
share any stories about hand-me-down recipes. You'll be
creating memories as well as sweet treats!

Treats from Mom's Kitchen

Strawberry-Rhubarb Crunch
Linda Diepholz
Lakeville, MN

I grew up eating rhubarb. Can't wait till it's in season and I can make something delicious! This fruit dessert is one of my favorites and it's super-simple to make.

1 c. sugar
3 T. all-purpose flour
3 c. fresh rhubarb, diced

1 c. fresh strawberries, hulled
and sliced
1 t. vanilla extract

Mix sugar and flour in a large bowl. Stir in rhubarb, strawberries and vanilla. Spoon mixture into an ungreased 13"x9" baking pan; sprinkle with Topping. Bake at 375 degrees for 45 minutes, or until golden. Serve warm. Makes 9 to 12 servings.

Topping:
1-1/2 c. all-purpose flour
1 c. brown sugar, packed

1 c. butter, softened

Mix flour and brown sugar in a bowl; cut in butter until crumbly.

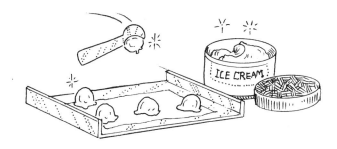

Serve up ice cream-topped desserts, the quick & easy way. Scoop ice cream ahead of time and freeze on a parchment paper-lined baking sheet.

Mom's Best
Sunday Suppers

Iowa Munchers

Violet Leonard
Chesapeake, VA

I'm not sure where these cookies got their name, but my mother made them at Christmas time along with many other goodies. They're too yummy not to make all year 'round!

1 c. butter, softened
1-1/2 c. brown sugar, packed
2 eggs
2 t. vanilla extract
2-1/2 c. all-purpose flour
1 t. baking powder
1/4 t. salt
1 c. pecans, finely chopped
1 c. milk chocolate chips
1/2 c. white chocolate chips
2/3 c. toffee baking bits, crushed

In a large bowl, blend butter and sugar. Beat in eggs, one at a time; stir in vanilla and set aside. In another bowl, combine flour, baking powder and salt; stir into butter mixture. Fold in remaining ingredients. Drop dough by tablespoonfuls onto lightly greased baking sheets. Bake at 350 degrees for 10 to 12 minutes, until lightly golden. Cool on baking sheets for 5 minutes; remove to wire racks and cool completely. Makes 2 dozen.

Peanut Butter Kiss Cookies

Kimberly Redeker
Savoy, IL

My mom started making this simple recipe a few years ago instead of the usual Peanut Blossom recipe, and we've never gone back. So simple and so tasty! Great recipe for kids to help with the kisses.

1 c. creamy peanut butter
1 egg, beaten
1 c. sugar
12 to 15 milk chocolate drops, unwrapped

In a bowl, mix together peanut butter, egg and sugar; roll into one-inch balls. Place on an ungreased baking sheet. Bake at 250 degrees for 6 to 7 minutes. Remove from oven; top each cookie with a chocolate drop. Cool completely. Makes 12 to 15 cookies.

Treats from Mom's Kitchen

Tin Roof Sundae Bars

Penny McShane
Lake in the Hills, IL

Loved by everyone...especially the wee ones! Love in your tummy!

18.3-oz. pkg. fudge brownie mix
1/2 c. very hot water
1/2 c. oil
1 egg, beaten

7-oz. jar marshmallow creme
1-1/2 c. salted peanuts
6 1.45-oz. chocolate candy bars,
 each bar broken in half

Grease the bottom of a 13"x9" baking pan very well; set aside. In a large bowl, combine brownie mix, hot water, oil and egg. Beat 50 strokes with a wooden spoon. Spread in prepared pan. Bake at 350 degrees for 30 to 35 minutes; do not overbake. Remove from oven; drop mounds of marshmallow creme over baked brownies. Wait several minutes and spread evenly. Sprinkle evenly with peanuts; top with candy bar pieces. Return to oven for 2 minutes. Remove from oven and spread chocolate evenly to cover. Refrigerate until chocolate is firm, about 2 hours. Cut into bars. Brownies cut easier after removing from refrigerator and standing at room temperature for 2 hours. Makes 3 dozen.

Once in a young lifetime, one should be allowed to have
as much sweetness as one can possibly want and hold.
–Judith Olney

Mom's Best
Sunday Suppers

Boston Cream Pie

Janis Parr
Ontario, Canada

This dessert is one of my family's favorites. It combines cake and custard with a rich chocolate frosting and is truly a decadent dessert.

18-1/2 oz. pkg. yellow cake mix
1 egg
1 egg white
1/2 c. sugar

1-1/2 T. cornstarch
1-1/4 c. cold milk
1 t. vanilla extract
1 t. butter

In a large bowl, prepare cake mix according to package directions. Pour batter into 2 greased 8" round cake pans. Bake at 350 degrees for 28 to 33 minutes; cool and set aside while preparing custard. In a small bowl, whisk together egg and egg white; set aside. In a small heavy saucepan, stir together sugar and cornstarch; whisk in cold milk. Over medium-low heat, cook and stir constantly until mixture starts to thicken. Whisk 2 tablespoons of hot mixture into eggs and then return it to the saucepan. Reduce heat to low; continue to stir constantly until mixture has thickened and bubbles break the surface. Remove from heat; stir in vanilla and butter. Pour custard into a bowl; cover and chill. To assemble, place one cake layer on a serving plate. Evenly spread cooled custard over top. Top with the second cake layer; cover only the top with Frosting. Chill; slice and serve cold. Serves 6 to 8.

Frosting:

1 c. powdered sugar
3 T. baking cocoa
1-1/2 T. hot water

1 t. butter
1 t. vanilla extract

In a small bowl, combine powdered sugar and cocoa; add hot water and stir well. Stir in butter and vanilla extract. Frosting will be thin.

Anchor layer cakes to serving plates with a dab of frosting... no more slipping and sliding.

Treats from Mom's Kitchen

Grandma Jean's Caramel Pecan Pie

Julia Graham
Sapulpa, OK

A caramel lover's dream! This pie is our family's most-requested recipe. It will be the star dessert for any gathering. You might need to make two pies, one to keep and one to share. Serves eight or one... we won't judge one bit!

28 caramel candies, unwrapped	1/2 t. vanilla extract
1/2 c. water	1/2 t. salt
1/4 c. butter	1 c. chopped pecans
2 eggs, beaten	9-inch pie crust, unbaked
3/4 c. sugar	Optional: pecan halves

Combine caramels, water and butter in a saucepan over low heat; cook until melted, stirring occasionally. Remove from heat; set aside. In a bowl, stir together eggs, sugar, vanilla and salt; fold in pecans. Add caramel mixture; stir well and pour into pie crust. If desired, arrange pecan halves on top. Bake at 400 degrees for 10 minutes. Reduce heat to 350 degrees; bake for an additional 30 minutes. Cool completely; cut into wedges. Makes 8 servings.

For a scrumptious dessert in a jiffy, make an ice cream pie! Soften 2 pints of your favorite ice cream and spread in a graham cracker crust, then freeze. Garnish with whipped topping and cookie crumbs or fresh berries.

Mom's Best
Sunday Suppers

Mom's Special Candy Cake

Sue Klapper
Muskego, WI

My mom used to make this special cake for our birthdays when we were young. To show you how old the recipe is, the original recipe called for a 29-cent bag of candies! I love the rich texture of the cake and, of course, the topping. Enjoy!

1-1/4 c. boiling water	2 eggs, beaten
1/2 c. chopped dates	1-1/2 c. all-purpose flour
1 t. baking soda	3 T. baking cocoa
1/2 c. butter, softened	1 t. baking powder
1 c. sugar	1 t. salt

In a large bowl, combine boiling water, dates and baking soda; mix well and let cool. In a separate bowl, blend butter, sugar and eggs; add to date mixture and set aside. In another bowl, sift flour, cocoa, baking powder and salt; add to batter and mix well. Spread batter in a greased 13"x9" baking pan; sprinkle Topping over batter. Bake at 350 degrees for 30 minutes, or until a toothpick inserted in center tests done. Cool; cut into squares and serve. Makes 16 servings.

Topping:

1/2 c. brown sugar, packed	6-oz. pkg. candy-coated
1/2 c. chopped nuts	chocolates

Combine all ingredients; mix well.

A little too much of a good thing is wonderful! Visit the baking department at your neighborhood craft store for mini candies and colorful sprinkles to dress up desserts in a jiffy.

Treats from Mom's Kitchen

Apple Cream Crumb Cake
Theresa Wehmeyer
Rosebud, MO

This easy, tasty apple treat is just the right size when you don't need a big dessert. Perfect with a cup of after-dinner coffee!

18-1/2 oz. pkg. yellow cake mix
1/4 c. butter, softened
2 eggs, divided
1 c. sour cream
21-oz. can apple pie filling
1/3 c. brown sugar, packed
1 t. cinnamon

In a large bowl, combine dry cake mix, butter and one egg; mix until crumbly. Reserve 1/2 cup of mixture for topping. Press remaining crumb mixture into a greased 8"x8" baking pan. In a small bowl, blend remaining egg with sour cream; spoon over crust. In another bowl, combine pie filling, brown sugar and cinnamon; spoon over sour cream mixture. Top with reserved crumb mixture. Bake at 350 degrees for 40 minutes, or until filling is bubbly and topping is lightly golden. Cool; cut into squares. Makes 9 servings.

Heavenly Strawberry Trifle
Pat Beach
Fisherville, KY

This is my family's all-time favorite summer dessert recipe. Besides being so, so yummy, it is also extremely easy to prepare and looks so pretty layered in a glass trifle bowl. If you like strawberry shortcake, you're going to love this simply delicious dessert!

1 lb. ripe strawberries, hulled
    and thinly sliced
13-1/2 oz. container strawberry
    glaze
14-oz. angel food cake, torn into
    bite-size pieces
9-oz. container frozen whipped
    topping, thawed

In a bowl, combine strawberries and strawberry glaze; mix together well. In a large glass bowl, layer 1/3 each of cake pieces, strawberry mixture and whipped topping. Repeat layering twice. Cover and refrigerate until serving time. Serves 6 to 8.

Mom's Best
Sunday Suppers

Mom's Baby Food Bars

Joyce Keeling
Springfield, MO

This recipe was given to my mom by my grandmother, and originally it called for strained prunes. Mom knew we kids would never touch anything with prunes in it, so she changed it to strained peaches. We loved them so much that they became a favorite dessert to take to every family function. What makes them so special is that you can substitute another flavor of baby food for an entirely different treat!

2 eggs	1 t. baking soda
1 c. sugar	1/2 t. salt
2 4-oz. jars peach baby food	1/2 c. oil
1 t. lemon extract	1/4 c. pecans, ground
1-1/2 c. all-purpose flour	Garnish: powdered sugar

In a large bowl, beat eggs until fluffy, gradually adding sugar. Add baby food and lemon extract; mix well. Sift flour, baking soda and salt into egg mixture and stir well. Stir in oil until well blended. Pour batter into a greased and floured 17"x12" jelly-roll pan; sprinkle with nuts. Bake at 350 degrees for 25 minutes, or until center springs back at a touch. Remove from oven; sprinkle with powdered sugar and let cool. Sprinkle again with powdered sugar; cut into bars. Makes 1-1/2 dozen.

Variations: Flavor of bars can be changed simply by changing flavors of baby food, using fruits like bananas, strawberry-banana, or sweet potato & squash. When using the sweet potato & squash, add a bit of cinnamon to the batter for a fall flavor.

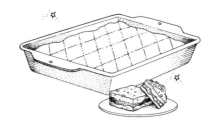

Bake up some cookie bars, then cut, wrap and freeze individually. Later, you can pull out just what you need for a spur-of-the-moment treat.

Treats from Mom's Kitchen

Strawberry Upside-Down Shortcake

Barb Bargdill
Gooseberry Patch

*I used to make this unusual recipe for my kids, years ago.
It's scrumptious...great for sharing!*

10-oz. pkg. mini marshmallows
18-1/4 oz. pkg. white cake mix
3-oz. pkg. strawberry gelatin mix
2 16-oz. pkgs. frozen sliced
   strawberries in syrup, thawed

8-oz. container frozen whipped
   topping, thawed

Spread marshmallows evenly in a greased 13"x9" baking pan; set aside. Prepare cake mix according to package instructions; pour batter over marshmallows in pan. Sprinkle dry gelatin mix over batter; cover with strawberries and syrup. Bake at 350 degrees for 50 minutes, or until a toothpick inserted in the center comes out clean. Let cool slightly. Run a knife around edge of pan; turn cake onto a serving tray. Cut into squares. Serve warm with whipped topping. Makes 15 servings.

Gather together your best-loved family recipes and share them on handmade recipe cards. Glue a color photo of your favorite relative in the corner of an index card, then write out her best-loved dessert recipe.

Lemon Icebox Dessert

Lynda Hart
Bluffdale, UT

In the late 40s and early 50s, my parents lived in a small town. For entertainment, three or four couples would get together and fix dinner. They called their little group the Met-N-Ett Club, country slang for Met and Ate. The club grew and continued meeting for many years. This dessert recipe was a favorite in the club.

12-oz. can evaporated milk
16 graham crackers, crushed
3 T. butter, melted
3-oz. pkg. lemon gelatin mix

3/4 c. hot water
1 c. sugar
1/4 c. lemon juice
2 T. lemon zest

Pour evaporated milk into a shallow container; freeze until slushy, about 30 minutes. In a bowl, mix graham cracker crumbs and melted butter; reserve 1/4 cup of mixture for topping. Press remaining crumb mixture into the bottom of an 8"x8" baking pan; cover and refrigerate. Meanwhile, in another bowl, dissolve gelatin in hot water. Stir in sugar, lemon juice and lemon zest. Cover and chill until thickened, but not set. Remove milk from freezer. Beat with an electric mixer on medium speed until soft peaks form; set aside. Beat thickened gelatin mixture on medium speed for about 2 minutes, until creamy; fold into the whipped milk. Spoon mixture over crumb crust; sprinkle with reserved crumb mixture. Cover and freeze for at least one hour. Remove from freezer about 20 minutes before serving; cut into squares. Serves 9.

Try a different kind of crumb crust for your favorite dessert. Simply replace graham crackers with vanilla wafers, shortbread cookies or gingersnaps...or use crushed pretzels for a tasty sweet & salty crust!

Fruit Cocktail Torte

Lisa Tucker
Dunbar, WV

*My grandmother gave me this recipe, and I have been making it
ever since, that's 40 years! It's a keeper...sweet and simple.*

1-1/2 c. all-purpose flour
1 c. sugar
1 t. baking soda
1 t. salt
15-oz. can fruit cocktail in syrup

1 egg, beaten
1/2 c. brown sugar, packed
1/2 c. chopped walnuts
Garnish: whipped topping

Combine flour, sugar, baking soda and salt in a large bowl; mix
together. Add fruit cocktail with syrup and egg. Spread batter evenly in
a greased 13"x9" baking pan; set aside. In a small bowl, combine brown
sugar and walnuts; sprinkle over batter. Bake at 350 degrees for 25 to
30 minutes. Cut into squares; serve with dollops of whipped topping.
Makes 10 servings.

Pure vanilla extract is a must in all kinds of baked treats!
If you do a lot of baking, save by purchasing a large bottle
of vanilla at a club store. Ounce for ounce, it's much
cheaper than buying the tiny bottles sold in the
supermarket baking aisle.

Mom's Best
Sunday Suppers

Dumplings in Apple Syrup

Joyce Keeling
Springfield, MO

This was one of my dad's favorite recipes that his mom made for a special treat when he was a boy in the early 1940s. It's become one of my favorites as well to serve on a cold winter evening. Grandma would sometimes pour a bit of cream over each serving. So good, and comforting.

3 Jonathan or Gala apples,
  peeled, cored and sliced
1-1/2 c. dark corn syrup
1 c. water

2 T. butter
2 4-inch cinnamon sticks,
  or 1/2 to 2 t. cinnamon
Optional: whipping cream

Make dough for Dumplings; set aside. Combine all ingredients except optional cream in a 10" or 12" cast-iron skillet over medium heat. Bring to a boil; continue boiling for 2 to 3 minutes, stirring occasionally. Drop tablespoonfuls of dough for Dumplings into boiling syrup. Reduce heat to medium-low; cover and simmer for 20 minutes. Do not lift lid while cooking. Remove from heat; discard cinnamon sticks, if using. Cool slightly and serve. May top with a little cream, if desired. Serves 6.

Dumplings:

1 c. all-purpose flour
2 t. baking powder
2 t. sugar
1 t. nutmeg

1/4 t. salt
1 egg, lightly beaten
1/3 c. milk

Sift together flour, baking powder, sugar, nutmeg and salt; set aside. Whisk together egg and milk; slowly fold into flour mixture.

There is nothing wrong with the world that a
sensible woman could not settle in an afternoon.
–Jean Giraudoux

Treats from Mom's Kitchen

Rowena's Pineapple Upside-Down Cake

Leona Krivda
Belle Vernon, PA

This recipe is a dessert my mom made often. My son Kevin loved this cake and was always so excited when she made it for him. I think that's why she made it so often. If you prefer, you can use pineapple rings instead of crushed pineapple. Arrange the rings in the pan over the brown sugar, then add the cherries inside the rings.

1/4 c. margarine, melted
1 c. brown sugar, packed
20-oz. can crushed pineapple,
   drained

10-oz. jar maraschino cherries,
   drained
15-1/4 oz. yellow cake mix
   with butter

Spread melted margarine in the bottom of a 13"x9" baking pan. Spread brown sugar evenly over margarine; spread pineapple evenly over brown sugar. Arrange cherries over pineapple; set aside. Prepare cake mix according to package directions; pour batter over ingredients in pan. Bake at 350 degrees for 40 to 45 minutes. Cool for 20 minutes; run a knife around edge of pan. Turn cake out of pan onto a platter. Cut into squares. Serves 10 to 12.

Mama's Raspberry-Mallow Pie

Judy Lange
Imperial, PA

Refreshing and light...a hit with everyone. You might just make two pies, because they go fast!

35 large marshmallows
1/2 c. milk
10-oz. pkg. frozen raspberries,
   thawed and mostly drained

8-oz. container frozen whipped
   topping, thawed
9-inch graham cracker crust

Combine marshmallows and milk in a large microwave-safe bowl. Microwave for one to 2 minutes; stir until smooth. Stir in raspberries; fold in whipped topping. Spoon mixture into crust. Cover and refrigerate for 2 hours or overnight; may also be frozen and served as a frozen pie. Cut into wedges. Serves 8.

Mom's Best
Sunday Suppers

Tres Leches Cake

Alejandra Ochoa
Pittsford, NY

My mother and I make this cake every year for my birthday. Usually, we decorate it with sliced mango or other fresh fruit on top, along with nuts or a sprinkle of cinnamon. This is a recipe we created together a few years ago.

1-1/2 c. all-purpose flour
1 t. baking powder
1/2 c. butter, softened
1 c. sugar
5 eggs

1/2 t. vanilla extract
2 c. whole milk
14-oz. can sweetened condensed
   milk
12-oz. can evaporated milk

Sift together flour and baking powder in a bowl; set aside. In another bowl, blend butter and sugar together until fluffy. Add eggs and vanilla; beat well. Add flour mixture to butter mixture, 2 tablespoons at a time; mix until well blended. Pour batter into a greased and floured 13"x9" baking pan. Bake at 350 degrees for 30 minutes, or until a toothpick inserted in the center tests done. Remove from oven; pierce cake all over with a fork. Combine milks in a separate bowl; pour over cooled cake. Cover and refrigerate for several hours. Spread Whipped Cream Frosting over cake; cut into squares. Keep refrigerated. Serves 8.

Whipped Cream Frosting:

1-1/2 c. whipping cream
1 c. powdered sugar

1 t. vanilla extract

Combine all ingredients in a large bowl. Beat with an electric mixer on medium-low speed until thickened.

Decorate cakes with sparkling sugared berries...simple! Brush berries with light corn syrup, then sprinkle generously with sanding sugar and allow to dry.

Treats from Mom's Kitchen

Brown Velvet Chocolate Cake

Cindy Neel
Gooseberry Patch

I enjoy looking at vintage magazines and I found this gem in a 1948 magazine. When I made it for my mom's birthday, it smelled so wonderful baking that my husband wanted me to make him one, too!

1-1/2 c. cake flour
1 t. baking soda
1/4 t. salt
1 c. buttermilk
1 c. sugar
1 egg, well beaten

2 sqs. unsweetened baking
  chocolate, melted
2 T. butter, melted
1 t. vanilla extract
Optional: favorite chocolate
  frosting

In a large bowl, sift together flour, baking soda and salt; set aside. In another bowl, combine buttermilk and sugar; stir until sugar is dissolved. Stir in egg; blend in melted chocolate and butter. Add flour mixture to buttermilk mixture; beat until well blended. Stir in vanilla. Pour batter into a greased 8"x8" baking pan. Bake at 350 degrees for 35 minutes, or until a toothpick inserted in the center comes out clean. Let cool; top with frosting, if desired. Makes 8 to 10 servings.

A little coffee brings out the flavor in any chocolate recipe.
Just dissolve a tablespoon of instant coffee granules in
liquid ingredients and continue as directed.

Mom's Best
Sunday Suppers

Lemon Pound Cake

Ida Mannion
North Chelmsford, MA

This pound cake is very tasty! My mom used to make it and it was always so good. Whenever I make this cake, it brings back nice memories of Mom in the kitchen, making good food and memories for us to treasure.

1/2 c. butter, softened	1/2 t. lemon extract
1 c. sugar	1-3/4 c. all-purpose flour
2 eggs	1/4 t. baking soda
1 t. lemon zest	1/2 t. salt
1 t. vanilla extract	

In a large bowl, beat butter and sugar until light and fluffy. Add eggs, one at a time, beating well after each addition. Beat in zest and extracts; set aside. In another bowl, whisk together flour, baking soda and salt. Gradually add to butter mixture, beating well. Pour batter into a greased and floured 9"x5" loaf pan. Bake at 350 degrees for 35 to 40 minutes, until a toothpick inserted in the center comes out clean. Cool cake in pan for 10 minutes; turn out onto a wire rack and cool completely. Spoon Lemon Icing over loaf; slice and serve. Makes 8 to 10 servings.

Lemon Icing:

3/4 c. powdered sugar	1 T. lemon juice
1/2 t. lemon zest	

Mix all ingredients until smooth.

Stir up an easy topping to spoon over pound cake. Mix a pint of sliced ripe strawberries with 1/4 cup strawberry jam and 1/4 cup orange juice...yummy!

Treats from Mom's Kitchen

Pistachio Delight

Peg Scott
Turtle Creek, PA

At Sunday dinner, there was always room for one or two more. My mom loved to cook and would invite people from church. She had so many recipes that took so little time to fix. You can substitute other flavors of pudding and fruit in this recipe.

8-oz. container frozen whipped
   topping, thawed
3.4-oz. pkg. instant pudding
   pistachio mix
1 c. mini marshmallows

11-oz. can pineapple tidbits,
   drained
11-oz. can mandarin oranges,
   drained

In a large bowl, whisk together whipped topping and dry pudding mix. Add marshmallows and fruit; mix well. Cover and refrigerate until chilled. Serves 6.

Mother's Ambrosia

Lisa Cunningham
Boothbay, ME

My mother's recipe is scrumptious...pretty in pink, perfect for a Mother's Day brunch or a baby shower! Simple to make, with just five ingredients.

20-oz. can crushed pineapple
8-oz. container frozen whipped
   topping, thawed
3.4-oz. pkg. instant vanilla
   pudding mix

1/2 of a 10-oz. pkg. mini
   marshmallows
8-oz. jar maraschino cherries,
   drained and 1/2 of juice
   reserved

In a large bowl, mix undrained pineapple and whipped topping; stir in dry pudding mix. Add marshmallows, cherries and reserved cherry juice; mix well. Cover and refrigerate at least 2 hours before serving. May be made up to 2 days ahead of time; stir again just before serving. Serves 10 to 12.

Brown Sugar Cookies

Melissa Bromen
Lake City, MN

These iced cookies have been a family favorite for decades! Mom would make them for the six of us siblings, and now we make them for our children and grandchildren. Always sure to bring smiles!

1 c. butter, softened	2 c. all-purpose flour
1/2 c. brown sugar, packed	1/2 t. baking soda
1/2 c. sugar	1 t. salt
1 egg, beaten	1/2 c. walnuts, finely ground
1 t. vanilla extract	Garnish: sugar for rolling

In a large bowl, combine all ingredients except garnish; mix well. Cover and chill dough for 20 minutes. Shape dough into small balls by teaspoonfuls; roll in sugar. Place cookies on ungreased baking sheets; press flat with the bottom of a glass. Bake at 350 degrees for 10 to 12 minutes, until golden. Cool cookies on wire racks; spread with warm Brown Sugar Icing. Reheat icing if it becomes too stiff to spread. Makes about 7 dozen.

Brown Sugar Icing:

1 c. brown sugar, packed	1 c. powdered sugar
1/2 c. whipping cream	

In a small saucepan; bring brown sugar and cream to a boil over medium heat. Boil for about 4 minutes, stirring until brown sugar dissolves. Remove from heat; beat in powdered sugar.

Line a pretty basket with one of Mom's vintage tea towels to deliver a special gift of cookies.

Treats from Mom's Kitchen

Old-Fashioned Buttermilk Pie

Amy Thomason Hunt
Traphill, NC

On Sundays at Grandma's, what could be more memorable or tasty than a buttermilk pie after a fried chicken dinner?

9-inch pie crust, unbaked
1/2 c. butter, softened
2 c. sugar
5 eggs

2 T. all-purpose flour
1 c. buttermilk
1 t. vanilla extract
juice of 1 lemon

Place pie crust in a 9" pie plate; set aside. In a large bowl, blend together butter and sugar. Add eggs, one at a time, blending thoroughly. Stir in flour, buttermilk, vanilla and lemon juice. Pour mixture into pie crust. Bake at 400 degrees for 10 minutes. Reduce temperature to 325 degrees; bake an additional 50 minutes, or until set. Cool completely; cut into wedges. Makes 6 to 8 servings.

When shopping for new cloth napkins, be sure to pick up an extra one. Use it to wrap around a flower pot, pitcher or pail and you'll always have a matching centerpiece.

Mom's Best
Sunday Suppers

Buttermilk Spice Cake

Judy Henfey
Cibolo, TX

This is an old recipe that my mother used to make. Frost with your favorite icing, or sprinkle with powdered sugar. Scrumptious with hot coffee or tea!

2 c. plus 2 t. all-purpose flour
1 c. sugar
1 t. baking powder
3/4 t. baking soda
1 t. salt
3/4 t. ground cloves

3/4 t. cinnamon
3/4 c. brown sugar, packed
1/2 c. shortening
1 c. buttermilk
3 eggs, beaten

In a large bowl, sift together flour, sugar, baking powder, baking soda, salt and spices. Add brown sugar, shortening and buttermilk. With an electric mixer on medium speed, beat for 2 minutes. Add eggs and beat another 2 minutes. Pour batter into 2 greased and floured 9" round cake pans, or one 13"x9" baking pan. Bake at 350 degrees for 35 to 40 minutes, until a toothpick tests done. Cool; turn out of pan(s). Serves 12 to 15.

Johnson White Cake Cookies

Kristin Pittis
Dennison, OH

I dug this old family recipe out of my grandma's recipe box. It was a recipe of her mother's. I can remember these cookies being on the dessert table at every family reunion when I was growing up.

1 c. shortening
1-1/2 c. sugar
1 c. milk
2 eggs, beaten
1 t. vanilla extract

2-1/2 c. all-purpose flour
2 t. baking powder
1/2 t. baking soda
1/8 t. salt
16-oz. can vanilla frosting

In a large bowl, blend together shortening and sugar. Stir in milk, eggs and vanilla; set aside. In another bowl, combine remaining ingredients except frosting; mix well and stir into shortening mixture. Drop dough by tablespoonfuls onto parchment paper-lined baking sheets. Bake at 350 degrees for 15 minutes, or until golden. Cool completely and frost. Makes 3 dozen.

Treats from Mom's Kitchen

Chocolatiest Chocolate Sauce *Karen Richardson*
Jarrettsville, MD

This chocolate sauce recipe was my grandmother's, and it was and still is served at every family gathering, which now includes my own grandchildren. Enjoy over ice cream or cake or any dessert calling for chocolate sauce. This is not a fudge sauce, so it is not meant to be thick. Grandmother always said to use the best brand of baking chocolate you could get.

6 T. hot water
2 sqs. unsweetened baking
   chocolate
1 T. butter

1/8 t. salt
1 c. sugar
3 T. corn syrup
1 t. vanilla extract

In a heavy saucepan over medium heat, combine hot water, chocolate, butter and salt. Slowly bring to a boil; add sugar and corn syrup. Boil for 2 to 3 minutes only. Allow to cool; stir in vanilla. May be made ahead, but don't bring to a boil, as sauce will become very stiff. Makes 10 servings.

Stock up on ice cream flavors, nuts and toppings...
spend an afternoon making banana splits
(and memories) with the kids!

Mom's Best
Sunday Suppers

Chocolate-Cinnamon Bars

Debbie Benzi
Binghamton, NY

My mother passed this recipe down to me. When I made it for my husband's family reunion, I received many requests for the recipe.

2 c. all-purpose flour
1 t. baking powder
1 c. sugar
1 T. cinnamon

1/2 c. margarine, softened
1/2 c. shortening
1 whole egg
1 egg, separated

In a large bowl, mix flour, baking powder, sugar and cinnamon. Add margarine, shortening, whole egg and egg yolk. Beat with an electric mixer on low speed until well blended. Pour batter into a greased 13"x9" baking pan; set aside. In another bowl, beat egg white lightly; spread over batter. Sprinkle with Topping. Bake at 350 degrees for 20 to 25 minutes. Cool; cut into squares. Serves 15.

Topping:

6-oz. pkg. semi-sweet
    chocolate chip
1/2 c. chopped walnuts

1/2 c. sugar
1 t. cinnamon

Combine all ingredients; toss to mix well.

For perfectly cut bar cookies and brownies, refrigerate them in the pan for about an hour after baking. Cut them with a plastic knife for a clean cut every time.

Treats from Mom's Kitchen

Joyce's Banana Dessert

Joyce Roebuck
Jacksonville, TX

I have taken this dessert to many occasions and it's always a hit with young and old. It's easy to make and so yummy! For variety, use bananas for one layer and juicy strawberries for the other layer.

2 c. whipping cream
2 T. sugar
15 chocolate sandwich cookies,
  crushed
4 ripe bananas, sliced

1/4 to 1/2 c. chopped pecans,
  toasted
Garnish: chocolate or
  caramel syrup

In a bowl, beat together cream and sugar with an electric mixer on high speed until stiff peaks form; set aside. In a large glass bowl or trifle dish, layer half each of crushed cookies, banana slices, pecans and whipped cream. Drizzle with syrup; repeat layers. Cover and chill until serving time. Makes 8 servings.

Mother's Pineapple Pie

Karen Thaler
Zephyrhills, FL

About 1995, my mother gave me this recipe because pineapple pie was one of my parents' favorite pies. There are other pineapple pie recipes, but none so easy to make and still taste great.

2 8-inch pie crusts, unbaked
20-oz. can crushed pineapple
2 T. all-purpose flour

2/3 c. sugar
2 T. lemon juice
1/8 t. salt

Fit one pie crust into an 8" pie plate; set aside. In a bowl, stir together pineapple with juice, flour and sugar. Stir in lemon juice and salt; pour into pie crust. Top with with remaining crust. Seal edges; make several slits with a knife tip. Bake at 400 degrees for 10 minutes. Reduce oven to 350 degrees and bake for for 15 minutes, or until crust is lightly golden. Cool; cut into wedges. Serves 8.

Mom's Best
Sunday Suppers

Cheesecake Supreme

Rosemary Trezza
Winter Springs, FL

This scrumptious recipe has been passed around in my family for many years. Once, a cousin made this cheesecake and brought it to my house. Another cousin was visiting at the time and was surprised to learn that this was the very cheesecake she always talked about! It has become a family favorite at holidays and special occasions.

5 8-oz. pkgs. cream cheese, room temperature	6 eggs, room temperature
1-1/4 c. sugar	2 t. vanilla extract
3 T. all-purpose flour	1/4 c. whipping cream

Prepare Graham Cracker Crust; refrigerate. In a large bowl, beat cream cheese with an electric mixer on medium speed until fluffy; set aside. In another bowl, mix together sugar and flour; gradually blend into cheese. Add eggs, one at a time, beating well after each egg. Add vanilla and cream; mix well. Pour into crust. Set on center rack of oven; bake at 500 degrees for 10 minutes. Reduce heat to 200 degrees; bake for one hour, or until center is firm. Let stand until cool; slice and serve. Serves 10.

Graham Cracker Crust:

1-1/4 c. graham cracker crumbs	1/4 c. butter, melted
1/4 c. sugar	

Mix together all ingredients. Press into a greased 9" or 10" springform pan, bringing mixture up along the sides. Refrigerate until needed.

Stir up a super-simple fruit topping. In a small bowl, combine a can of fruit pie filling and 2 tablespoons orange juice. Microwave for 2 to 2-1/2 minutes, stirring twice; serve warm.

Treats from Mom's Kitchen

Pecan Squares

Susan Young
Mount Victory, OH

This recipe is from an old, old cookbook received when Mom was a new bride. So quick, easy and good!

2 eggs
1 c. brown sugar, packed
1/2 c. pecan pieces
1/2 c. all-purpose flour

1/3 c. butter, melted
1 t. vanilla extract
Optional: caramel frosting

Beat eggs in a large bowl; add brown sugar, then pecans. Add flour, melted butter and vanilla; mix well. Pour into a greased 9"x9" baking pan. Bake at 350 degrees for 25 minutes, or until golden. Cool; spread with frosting, if desired. Cut into squares. Makes 16 servings.

If your baked dessert didn't turn out quite the way you expected, layer it with whipped cream in a parfait glass and give it a fancy name. It will still be scrumptious... and nobody will know the difference!

Mom's Best
Sunday Suppers

Italian Cream Cake

Courtney Stultz
Weir, KS

This is my mother's recipe, with just a few modifications. She loves this cake and I'm so happy she shared the recipe with me. It features a sweet vanilla cake with pecans and coconut, topped with cream cheese frosting.

2/3 c. shortening or butter
1-1/2 c. sugar
5 eggs, separated
2 c. all-purpose flour
1 t. baking soda

1 c. buttermilk
1 t. vanilla extract
1 c. flaked coconut, divided
1/2 c. chopped pecans, divided

In a large bowl, beat together shortening or butter and sugar until smooth. Add egg yolks and beat well; set aside. In another bowl, combine flour, baking soda, buttermilk and vanilla; add to shortening mixture and stir well. Gently mix in half each of coconut and pecans; set aside. In a separate bowl, beat egg whites until light and fluffy; fold into batter. Pour into 2 greased 9" round cake pans. Bake at 350 degrees for 25 to 30 minutes, until a toothpick tests clean. Remove from oven and let cool for about 10 minutes. Carefully remove cakes from pans; cool completely on wire racks. Place one cake on a serving plate; spread thinly with Cream Cheese Frosting. Top with remaining cake; frost top and sides. Sprinkle remaining coconut and pecans on top. Slice and serve. Makes 10 servings.

Cream Cheese Frosting:

8-oz. pkg cream cheese, softened   2 c. powdered sugar

In a bowl, with an electric mixer using whisk attachment, beat cream cheese and powdered sugar on medium speed until smooth and whipped, about 2 minutes.

Garnish desserts with a strawberry fan...so pretty! Starting at the tip, cut a strawberry into thin slices almost to the stem. Carefully spread slices to form a fan.

Treats from Mom's Kitchen

Sunday Coconut Cake

Gladys Kielar
Whitehouse, OH

Every Sunday, we visited my Aunt Mary. She always had
this delicious coconut cake ready for our visit.

18-1/4 oz. pkg. yellow cake mix
1-1/2 c. milk
1/2 c. sugar

2 c. flaked coconut, divided
8-oz. container frozen whipped
topping, thawed

Prepare and bake cake mix as directed on package, using a greased
13"x9" baking pan. Set pan on a wire rack to cool for 15 minutes; use
a fork to poke holes down throughout cake. Meanwhile, in a saucepan,
combine milk, sugar and 1/2 cup coconut; bring to a boil over medium-
high heat. Reduce heat to low and simmer for one minute. Carefully
spoon hot milk mixture over warm cake; allow liquid to soak down
through holes. Cool completely. In another bowl, fold 1/2 cup remaining
coconut into whipped topping; spread over cooled cake. Sprinkle
remaining coconut over cake; chill. Cut into squares and serve. Makes
8 servings.

Toasted coconut makes a scrumptious dessert topper. Simply
spread shredded coconut on an ungreased baking sheet.
Bake at 350 degrees for 5 to 7 minutes.

INDEX

Breads

6-Week Bran Muffins, 165
Amish White Bread, 159
Apple Spice Muffins, 150
Beckie's Corn Muffins, 151
Beer Mustard Biscuits, 174
Cheddar Beer Rolls, 171
Cheesy Cheddar Twists, 175
Cheesy French Bread, 167
Cranberry-Walnut Muffins, 164
Dilly Casserole Bread, 154
Double-Quick Dinner Rolls, 176
Family-Favorite Focaccia Bread, 162
Garden Bruschetta, 161
Gram's Angel Biscuits, 179
Grand-Aunt's Grecian Bread, 170
Grandma Truda's Zucchini Bread, 169
Grandma's Best Banana-Walnut
 Bread, 180
Lemon Cream Biscuits, 173
Lisa's Italian-Seasoned Flatbread, 166
Mamma Char's Buttermilk Biscuits, 179
Mom's Biscuits, 156
Mom's Mexican Bread, 151
No-Fail Potato Rolls, 152
Old-Fashioned Garlic Bread, 177
Old-Fashioned Icebox Yeast Rolls, 172
Pineapple Date Loaf, 168
Quick Rolls, 171
Root Beer Rye Bread, 165
Simple & Delicious Dinner Rolls, 155
Streusel-Topped Blueberry Muffins, 158
Sun-Dried Tomato Bread, 160
Sweet Thin Skillet Cornbread, 163
Tried & True Honey Oat Bread, 149
Yeast Dinner Rolls, 148

Condiments

30-Minute Apple Butter, 178
Apricot Freezer Jam, 157
Chocolatiest Chocolate Sauce, 211
Cinnamon Honey Butter, 157
Fresh Herb Butter, 153
Herb Garden Butter, 177
Lemon & Chive Butter, 161
Strawberry Microwave Jam, 178

Cookies

Aunt Roxie's Sugar Cookies, 187
Brown Sugar Cookies, 208
Chocolate-Cinnamon Bars, 212
Coconut-Pecan Squares, 186
Iowa Munchers, 192
Johnson White Cake Cookies, 210
Mom's Baby Food Bars, 198
Peanut Butter Kiss Cookies, 192
Pecan Squares, 215
Tin Roof Sundae Bars, 193

Desserts

Apple Cream Crumb Cake, 197
Aunt Eula's Oatmeal Pie, 182
Boston Cream Pie, 194
Brown Velvet Chocolate Cake, 205
Buttermilk Spice Cake, 210
Cheesecake Supreme, 214
Citrus Delight Bundt® Cake, 184
Dumplings in Apple Syrup, 202
Fresh Fruit Kuchen, 189
Fruit Cocktail Torte, 201
Grandma Jean's Caramel Pecan
 Pie, 195
Heavenly Strawberry Trifle, 197
Italian Cream Cake, 216
Joyce's Banana Dessert, 213
Lemon Icebox Dessert, 200
Lemon Pound Cake, 206
Mama's Raspberry-Mallow Pie, 203
Mom's Bread Pudding, 185
Mom's Special Candy Cake, 196
Mother's Ambrosia, 207
Mother's Pineapple Pie, 213
Old-Fashioned Buttermilk Pie, 209
Peach-Blueberry Crumble, 190
Perfect Peach Cobbler, 183
Pistachio Delight, 207
Poppy's Sour Cream Apple Pie, 188
Rowena's Pineapple Upside-Down
 Cake, 203
Strawberry Upside-Down Shortcake, 199
Strawberry-Rhubarb Crunch, 191
Sunday Coconut Cake, 217
Tres Leches Cake, 204

INDEX

INDEX

Find Gooseberry Patch
wherever you are!

www.gooseberrypatch.com

Call us toll-free at 1·800·854·6673

U.S. to Metric Recipe Equivalents

Volume Measurements

1/4 teaspoon	1 mL
1/2 teaspoon	2 mL
1 teaspoon	5 mL
1 tablespoon = 3 teaspoons	15 mL
2 tablespoons = 1 fluid ounce	30 mL
1/4 cup	60 mL
1/3 cup	75 mL
1/2 cup = 4 fluid ounces	125 mL
1 cup = 8 fluid ounces	250 mL
2 cups = 1 pint =16 fluid ounces	500 mL
4 cups = 1 quart	1 L

Weights

1 ounce	30 g
4 ounces	120 g
8 ounces	225 g
16 ounces = 1 pound	450 g

Oven Temperatures

300° F	150° C
325° F	160° C
350° F	180° C
375° F	190° C
400° F	200° C
450° F	230° C

Baking Pan Sizes

Square

8x8x2 inches	2 L = 20x20x5 cm
9x9x2 inches	2.5 L = 23x23x5 cm

Rectangular

13x9x2 inches	3.5 L = 33x23x5 cm

Loaf

9x5x3 inches	2 L = 23x13x7 cm

Round

8x1-1/2 inches	1.2 L = 20x4 cm
9x1-1/2 inches	1.5 L = 23x4 cm